D1247101

*Black Women
in the Labor Force*

Black Women
in the Labor Force

Phyllis A. Wallace

with Linda Datcher
and Julianne Malveaux

The MIT Press
Cambridge, Massachusetts, and London, England

331.4
W19b

© 1980 by
The Massachusetts Institute of Technology

All rights reserved. No part of this book may be reproduced in any form or by any means, electronic or mechanical, including photocopying, recording, or by any information storage and retrieval system, without permission in writing from the publisher.

This book was set in Helvetica by ALLIED SYSTEMS – Div. of Frank Thompson Assoc., Inc. and printed and bound by The Murray Printing Company in the United States of America.

Library of Congress Cataloging in Publication Data

Wallace, Phyllis Ann.
    Black women in the labor force.

    Bibliography: p.
    Includes index.
    1. Afro-American women — Employment. I. Datcher, Linda, joint author. II. Malveaux, Julianne, joint author. III. Title.
HD6057.5.U5W34   331.4'11   80-14175
ISBN 0-262-23103-4

LMS

To My Parents

JAN 5 '81

UNIVERSITY LIBRARIES
CARNEGIE-MELLON UNIVERSITY
PITTSBURGH, PENNSYLVANIA 15213

Contents

1

Introduction   1

2

Labor Force Participation of Black Women: A Review of the Economic Literature   10

3

Selected Supply Characteristics of Black Women Workers   23

7
Conclusions

Appendix A

Appendix B

List of Tables

List of Figures

Preface

This survey of recent economic literature on the employment status of black women is an attempt to fit a number of contradictory findings into a more comprehensible context. The task became far more difficult than was originally indicated by the nature of the research. Perhaps this is an indication that economists and other social scientists need to coordinate their research in this area.

Some financial support was received from the National Council On Employment Policy and the Industrial Relations Section of the Alfred P. Sloan School of Management at MIT. Although I have asked several colleagues to review this report, I am solely responsible for its perspective. I am grateful to Bernard Anderson, Carolyn Shaw Bell, Marcia Freedman, Bennett Harrison, Annette LaMond, Kenneth Mericle, Pauli Murray, Charles A. Myers, and Barbara Reagan for reviewing this report. Two young black women economists who have earned Ph.D.s in economics at MIT, Linda Datcher and Julianne Malveaux, have prepared essays that are included here. Some of the issues raised in this study may be a source of debate and controversy for years, and we welcome new researchers.

Irene Goodsell and Joyce Yearwood typed the numerous revisions and final draft of this manuscript, and Cynthia Palmer prepared the charts and checked the statistical tables.

*Black Women
in the Labor Force*

1

Introduction

Research for this study was started several years ago with a survey of the economic literature on the employment status of black women during the 1960–1970 decade. It soon became apparent that, although a number of economists had conducted studies on the labor force participation (LFP) of women, few had focused on the distinctive characteristics of black women in the civilian labor force. Thus the economic literature is particularly sparse on this topic.

The existing economic literature on black women in the labor force suffers from two shortcomings. The first deficiency might be termed the macro-micro dichotomy. In comparing the relative occupational position and relative incomes of black women with their white female counterparts, economists have tended to employ macroanalysis and sophisticated methologies for handling massive amounts of data. Their findings are full of paradoxes, and for this reason we attempt to illuminate some of the inconsistencies by a more critical analysis of microdata. For example, the sections of this report that examine the decline of the occupational category "domestic worker" as a mainstay of black women workers or the special problems of black female teenage workers and black women who head families provide a sharper focus for some of the aggregate research findings. Both research strategies, of course, are necessary in order to understand the labor market behavior of black women.

A second deficiency is that although many social science researchers claim objectivity, their personal value systems intrude on the analysis. To some extent their findings are distorted not only by sins of misspecification of economic models but, more important, by unwarranted inferences from

Throughout this report the term black has been used, and depending on the source of the data it may cover nonwhites (over 90 percent are blacks) or blacks only.

rigorous analysis; for example, the tendency to speculate about the psychosociological characteristics of individuals, the inheritance of economic status, or the structure of black families.

Essentially, in this report we are concerned about black women, both employed and unemployed, in the civilian labor force. The tremendous attention that has been devoted to black women outside of the labor market, especially those in the welfare system, has tended to obscure employment issues. We differentiate between the employment system and the welfare system in the following way: "The employment system provides opportunities for remunerative work in both the private and public sectors . . . The welfare system is intended to provide some minimum standard of adequacy of consumption for some persons, who for various reasons, are not receiving sufficient income from other sources."[1] The welfare system might be classified as one segment of a transfer system that also includes employment-related social and private insurance to replace earnings lost due to unemployment, disability, retirement, or death. Bennett Harrison's recent study of the relationship between work and welfare found that "mixing of work and welfare was more prevalent among minority households: between 11.4 percent and 16.4 percent mixed wages and income from welfare in any one year, and that one out of every three mixed work and public assistance over the course of the five years [1968–1972]."[2]

The primary objective of this report is to provide information on a significant segment of minority workers as well as produce some insights on the better utilization of *all* women in the labor market. (See figure 1.1.) Black women workers, more so than white women, have had a dual role as contributors to family income, often as primary wage earners. The main reason for the historically high number of black women in the labor force has been the large gap between the family incomes of blacks and whites. In 1976 black wives made a substantial contribution to the income of their families. The median income (earnings plus other money income)

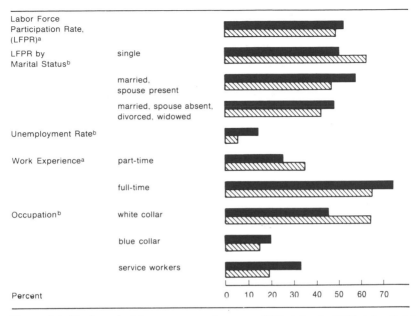

Labor Force Participation Rate, (LFPR)[a]		
LFPR by Marital Status[b]	single	
	married, spouse present	
	married, spouse absent, divorced, widowed	
Unemployment Rate[b]		
Work Experience[a]	part-time	
	full-time	
Occupation[b]	white collar	
	blue collar	
	service workers	
Percent		0 10 20 30 40 50 60 70

Figure 1.1 Black and white women workers. a. 1976 data. b. 1978 data. Solid bars represent black women; shaded bars represent white women. See tables 2.1, 3.1, 4.1, R.4, and R.9 for statistics.

of black husband/wife families with wives in the paid labor force was $15,744, or 60 percent higher than median income for black families with the husband as the only wage earner. The median income for white husband/wife families with wives in the paid labor force was $17,922, or 21 percent higher than white families with the husband as the only wage earner. Black families headed by women had median incomes that were only one-third the size of black husband/wife family incomes with both spouses working and slightly more than half the median income of black husband/wife families with the husband as the only wage earner.[3]

The option of market work versus home work and/or leisure is a luxury that few black married women have enjoyed. Overwhelming economic reasons for supporting and sustaining the family have kept them in the work force. Traditionally, the labor force participation of black married women, regardless of the presence of young children, age, education, occupation, and income of husband, has been high and continuous. Few black married women workers have faced the re-entry problems of older white women who were absent from the labor force during their childbearing and child rearing years, although the male-female earnings gap has been attributed by some mainly to this discontinuity of work experience.[4]

Much of the economic and statistical data on black women workers is also subsumed in studies of black/white economic differences. An examination of the labor market experiences of black women becomes an exercise in how to disentangle the effects of race and sex. Black women have had different labor market experiences than white women when comparisons are made along sex lines, and they differ significantly in work behavior from black males when comparisons are made along racial lines. The interaction of race and sex may jeopardize their labor market status.

In the past the combination of race and sex discrimination has meant the almost complete isolation of black women workers from the internal labor markets or segregation into submarkets. Black women have been concentrated in the most menial, low-paying, and most unrewarding occupations in the general labor market or have served minority clients in segregated markets as teachers, social workers, nurses, and librarians. However, the recent upgrading of the occupational status of black women workers as well as their broader work experience in a number of labor markets have improved their relative economic status.

Labor market characteristics as well as personal characteristics are important in shaping the labor force participation of minorities and women. Many minority group members seek employment in markets within which most individuals are employed. Preferred workers may be well endowed with education and training, and in the primary markets where they are employed, there are opportunities for promotion, security, and high wages. Workers in secondary labor markets face far less attractive opportunity structures and experience more unemployment. Historically, blacks have been restricted to these secondary labor markets with limited chances to shift to primary labor markets. Even when blacks have invested heavily in human capital (education, training) and otherwise sought to improve their earnings, they have been accorded differential treatment because of attributes not associated with productivity.

The assessment of individual workers on the basis of average characteristics of the groups to which they belong (that is, perceptions of employers based on other than individual characteristics) restricts labor market options for minorities and women. This statistical discrimination adversely affects the employment status and earnings potential of black women workers. We want to know why the significant differences between black and white women workers remain even after controlling for such factors as educational attainment, marital status, presence of children, and other family income. Beyond this, the major comparisons must be of black women workers versus all participants in the labor force.

We were surprised by the large number of conflicting ob servations on the labor market behavior of black women. Even when researchers utilize the same data bases, such as the decennial census materials or the Current Population Survey, the admonition that the coefficients of a multiple regression are no better than the specification of the model that has yielded them[5] needs to be underscored.* At other times, however, the problem appears to lie with the tools of

---

*Regression analysis is a statistical technique used to test hypotheses derived from economic theory about the significance of particular variables. For example, to explain the variation in labor force participation, the dependent variable, we should account for as many independent variables as possible. Thus education, other family income, children, and marital status may be the major explanatory factors. Coefficients are the estimators of the variables.

analysis. As yet, sociological and psychological attitudinal variables have not been incorporated into the neoclassical labor supply models. This is unfortunate because black women workers do not seem to fit easily into the conventional economic mold. Another problem arises because the normative stance in social science research on relative occupational status has been to compare minority women to white women. This procedure tends to obscure the fact that although black women have experienced dramatic rises in their employment status relative to white women, white women have been concentrated into jobs that are at the lower end of the occupational hierarchy. Within occupational groups, however, black women are concentrated at the lower skill range of the occupations.

This report is an initial building block, a survey of completed economic research. Other researchers may undertake more in-depth and searching analysis. If resources are available, far more sophisticated techniques might be used on a wealth of information. If we can survey and dissect one small area, others might be encouraged to undertake interdisciplinary approaches to explain the less than satisfactory experience of black women in the labor markets of this country.

Although the central focus of this report is on changes in the employment status of black women after 1960, a brief summary of the historical status of black women workers is pertinent. Black women have always comprised a significant proportion of the black labor force. This percentage increased from about a third at the beginning of the century to 47 percent in 1978. Black women workers as a percentage of the female work force, however, decreased from 22 percent in 1910 to 14 percent in 1978. (See table 1.1.) Black women workers are now approximately 6 percent of the civilian labor force.*

---

*The official definition of the civilian labor force includes only those who are employed or seeking employment, not discouraged workers, that is, persons who are no longer looking for work because they believe no suitable work is available.

Table 1.1 Black (and Other Nonwhite) Women in the Labor Force, 1910–1978

Year	Number (× 1,000)	Percentage of Black Workers	Percentage of Women Workers
1910	1,613	33.9	21.7
1920	1,631	32.3	18.9
1930	1,841	33.4	17.1
1940	1,843	32.8	14.3
1950	2,086	34.3	12.7
1960	3,046	39.8	13.1
1970	4,015	43.6	12.7
1975	4,795	45.5	13.0
1977	5,266	46.6	13.2
1978	5,679	47.5	13.6

Sources: For 1910–1960, Dale Hiestand, *Economic Growth and Employment Opportunities for Minorities,* p. 7. For 1970–1978, U.S. Department of Labor, Employment and Training Administration, *Employment and Training Report of the President,* 1979, Table A-3.

Perhaps the more interesting story is the shift in the occupational position of black women. (The index of relative occupational position, an aggregate measure devised by Gary Becker, compares the occupational distribution of black women relative to white women. Between 1910 and 1960 this index increased from 78.0 to 84.3.[6]) In 1910, 60 percent of the black female labor force was nonfarm workers, of whom 95 percent were classified as semiskilled workers, laborers, and service workers. By 1960 the nonfarm total accounted for 94 percent of the black female work force, and semiskilled workers, laborers, and service workers were 80 percent of the nonfarm total.[7] In 1940 about 60 percent of the 1.5 million employed black women worked in the lowest-paying jobs as private household workers, but by 1960 only 36 percent of the employed black women were in this occupation. The major industrial shift for black women workers up to 1960 was from agricultural to nonfarm jobs, and the significant occupational shift after 1940 was from household worker to clerical and other white-collar jobs.

As compared to white after 1940—

(The post-1960 period is selected for review of the employment status of black women both because of the enormous changes that occurred as well as the abundance of data available.) The relative economic status of black women was greatly improved between 1960 and 1970 because of three fundamental changes in their labor force participation: the shift from part-time to full-time employment; the impressive decline in the proportion of black women employed as household workers, from more than 33 percent in 1960 to less than 14 percent in 1970; and increased convergence in the job structures of black women as compared with white women, evidenced by the large differences in productivity characteristics between entering and retiring cohorts in the labor market.)

The survey of the major economic literature on the labor force participation of black women is presented in chapter 2. Labor force participation studies of women have focused on the largest group of such workers, married with spouse present (MSP). In 1978 nearly three out of every five white women workers and two out of every five black women workers were classified in this group. Although the choice between market work and nonmarket activities as a determinant of labor supplied to the market has been confirmed for working wives in general, black wives may give more weight to monetary compensation because the earnings profile for black husbands is significantly lower than for white husbands.

The economic literature on the labor force participation of women has emphasized the role of married women with spouse present, but black women workers in other categories—married with spouse absent, single, divorced, and widowed—experience major difficulties in labor markets. These other categories account for 60 percent of black women workers and 42 percent of white women workers. Nearly a quarter of black women workers are heads of families. Only recently, as welfare reform has emerged as a major policy issue, has some interest been paid to this segment of the work force.

A large number of economic studies have been surveyed in order to assess other characteristics of black women workers. Chapter 3 examines their occupational status, work schedules, educational attainment, and age and the effect of the presence of children. Chapter 4 reviews the impact of labor market policies, such as employment and training programs and antidiscrimination efforts, as techniques for improving the labor market experience of black women. Chapter 5 assesses the black/white earnings differential from the perspective of black women workers. Chapter 6 highlights the employment status of two especially disadvantaged groups of black women workers: teenagers and female heads of families. Also, a more detailed study is made of the private household service occupation, in which the largest number of black women were employed, at least until 1960. Structural changes in the labor market in the following decade induced a major shift of black women out of this occupation. In chapter 7 some research issues for future efforts are outlined and some policy implications are noted. A number of reference tables have been included in appendix A, and data sources are noted in appendix B.

Although it might appear that undue attention is given to technical issues in this report, the context is much larger. The economic status of blacks, the largest minority group in the United States, is our major concern.[8] Many studies have recommended a much larger investment in education and training as the way to increase the economic well-being of blacks. Other studies have emphasized affirmative action programs to reduce employment discrimination. Given their low relative standing in the labor market, black women workers would benefit from a mix of programs.

2

Labor Force Participation of Black Women: A Review of the Economic Literature

Labor force participation rates are one of the most important dimensions of activity in the labor market. The percentage of the female population over 16 years of age employed in a variety of occupations and industries or seeking employment in the civilian labor force reveals much about the personal and family characteristics of workers as well as their response to labor market structures. There were 4.7 million black women in the civilian labor force in March 1978. Approximately 46 percent of these women still lived in the South. (See table R.1.) Forty percent of all black women in the labor force were married with spouse present, 30 percent were single, and 30 percent were separated, divorced, or widowed. (See tables R.2 and R.3.)

Traditionally labor force participation rates for black women have been higher than for white women, but by 1978 the gap had narrowed considerably because of the rising white female participation, mainly by married women. Over the past 25 years the labor force participation rate for white women has increased by about 15 percentage points compared to 5 percentage points for black women. The participation rate for black women in the civilian labor force in March 1978 was 52.2 percent compared with 48.6 percent for white women. (See table 2.1.) There was great variation by age groups, ranging from exceedingly low levels for black teenagers to well over 60 percent for black women workers between 25 and 44 years of age. (See table R.4 and figure 2.1.)

Comparison of the labor force participation rates for black and white women by marital status in 1978 reveals that black wives have higher rates than white wives, and a sizeable gap exists between labor force participation rates for single black and white women workers. This disparity is greatest for

Table 2.1 Labor Force Participation Rates of Women by Marital Status, March 1978

Marital Status	Black	White
Single	49.9	62.7
Married		
spouse present	58.3	46.6
spouse absent	56.2	56.8
Divorced	66.3	75.1
Widowed	27.2	21.6
Total	52.2	48.6

Source: U.S. Department of Labor, Bureau of Labor Statistics, *Marital and Family Characteristics of the Labor Force,* March 1978.

women between 16 and 24 years of age. Although black wives with spouse absent have participation rates as high as their white counterparts, the former group makes up 13 percent of black women workers whereas the latter group makes up only 4 percent of the white women workers. Many of the black women heads of families fall within the poverty group. There is considerable dispute within the economic literature on the significance of the black/white differentials on labor force participation, and several major studies that are reviewed here reflect this.

The conceptual models that underlie economic research on the labor force participation of married women have been formulated in terms of allocation of time between market (paid labor force) and nonmarket activities (home work and leisure) and within the context of production in the home (children, household activities). These economic models rely on standard consumption theory; that is, households attempt to maximize utility over the life cycle and will consume commodities in accordance with their permanent (or long-run) income. The family is seen as the major economic unit making a number of joint household decisions on consumption, allocation of production, and investment, especially in the human capital of its members. The decision of married women to divide their time between market and nonmarket

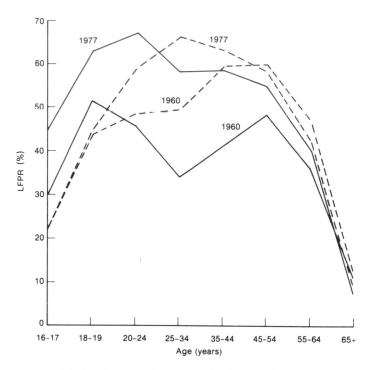

Figure 2.1 Labor force participation rates (LFPR) of women by age, 1960 and 1978. Dotted lines represent black women; solid lines represent white women. See table R.4 for statistics.

activities is affected by variables such as other family income, educational achievement, presence of children, race, age, and market wages.[1]

In 1960 Jacob Mincer, in a path-breaking analysis of the labor force participation of white married women, found that the most important variable with respect to the market/nonmarket tradeoff was the female wage rate. The supply of married women workers responded to an increase in market wages through a large substitution effect (increase of hours offered in the labor market). The wage variable had a more powerful effect than the husband's income. Mincer hypothesized that a transitory change in the income of the family had a stronger effect on the labor force participation of married women than did an equivalent change in permanent income. Thus an apparent contradiction between the market behavior of wives as a result of a rise in family income (expected decline in labor force participation) and their market activity as a result of a rise in their wages (expected increase in labor force participation) could be reconciled.[2]

Mincer's model excluded black married women who, at a given moment, had a higher propensity to work and, for the most part, received relatively less attractive wages. Cain stated that this "puzzle provided the initial incentive for (his) study on work" by both black and white wives.

There is considerable dispute within the economic literature on the significance of this differential, and the five major studies that are reviewed next reflect this lack of scholarly consensus. In addition to these primary studies, this chapter reflects the results of an intensive survey of economic literature, as listed in the bibliography.

Cain

Cain's examination of the differences between the labor force behavior of black and white married women, _Married Women In the Labor Force,_ expanded the conceptual framework that Mincer developed for white women. The intriguing questions for Cain were why labor force participation among black wives was higher at any given time than for white women and why the presence of children did not inhibit work by black wives. An economic model of labor force participation of married women was tested by regression analysis utilizing a variety of data for the period 1940–1960. The secular rise in the labor force participation of married women was determined mainly by the positive effect of the rise in real wages that exceeded the negative effect of the rise in incomes.[3] Thus married women were attracted to the paid work force from nonmarket activities. Educational attainment had a positive effect and the presence of children had a negative effect on the labor force participation of wives.

UNIVERSITY LIBRARIES
CARNEGIE-MELLON UNIVERSITY
PITTSBURGH, PENNSYLVANIA 15213

Although the labor force behavior of black wives was similar to white wives, Cain observed some important differences: a slower rate of increase, over time, in the labor force participation of black wives; higher levels of labor force participation of black wives on a cross-sectional basis; and a weaker effect of the presence of children on the work behavior of black wives. His explanations for these differences were the greater prevalence of part-time work by black wives, which permitted easier scheduling of child care; poorer housing conditions facing black families, which induced more market work by black wives; greater marital instability of black families; and greater employment discrimination against black husbands than black wives, which led to a substitution in market work between them.[4] Cain presented no evidence concerning the effect of crowding and the low quality of housing and did not develop the discussion on discrimination against black husbands.[5]

By 1976, Cain and Dooley had developed a more sophisticated model of labor supply, the fertility decision (whether to have children), and wages of married women. Their empirical results based on 1970 census data supported earlier research findings that for black wives the positive wage effects tended to be offset by the negative effect of other family income.[6]

Bowen and Finegan

In a comprehensive analysis of labor force participation rates for several demographic groups, including married women (14–54 years old), single women (25–54 years old), older women (55 years old and over) and younger women (14–24 years old), Bowen and Finegan used cross-sectional and trend data for the post-war period, 1948–1965, in *The Economics of Labor Force Participation*. According to their calculations, about half of the 12.3 differential in the labor force participation rates of black and white married women in 1960 disappeared when adjustment was made for the effects of age and schooling of the wife, the presence of children, employment status of the husband, and other family income.* In their regression analysis, the adjusted rate for black wives was 42.0, or only 6.8 percentage points higher than the adjusted participation rates for white married women.[7] The authors concluded that "The fact that the participation rate of Negro married women is still almost 7 points higher than the participation rate of white married women after we have allowed for these demographic and economic differences is at least as important as the finding that a comparison of unadjusted participation rates exaggerates the effect of color per se on participation . . . Taking account of the tendency for Negro married women to work shorter hours than a comparable group of white women brings about a further reduction in the gap between the Negro and white participation rates . . . the final differential being 3.1 points."[8] Thus the typical black married woman allocated 10 percent rather than 35 percent more time to the labor market during the census week of 1960 than a comparable white woman.** Although black women may work fewer hours, they may desire to work more hours.

The following are other major findings of the Bowen-Finegan study as it pertains to racial differences in labor force participation rates of married women.

The adjusted labor force participation rate for black wives with children under six is considerably higher than such rates for white women with children under six;

The adjusted participation rate for black married women with 16 or more years of school completed is extraordinarily high (83 percent);

---

*Unadjusted labor force participation rates were 47.0 for black wives and 34.7 for white wives (47.0 − 34.7 = 12.3); adjusted rates were 42.0 and 35.2 for blacks and whites, respectively.

**47.0/34.7 = 1.35 for unadjusted rates, 42.0/35.2 = 1.19 for adjusted rates, and 34.5/31.4 = 1.10 for adjustment to full-time–equivalent participants.

The participation rate for black married women appears to be considerably less sensitive to differences in other family income than does the participation rate for all married women. "So long as other family income is below some threshold level, the pressure on the wife to work leaves little scope for the substitution effect" (market/nonmarket tradeoff).[9]

Although Bowen and Finegan seem puzzled by the lack of sensitivity of the labor force participation rates of black wives to other family income, educational attainment below the college level, and the differential gains in access to more desirable jobs, they make no attempt to associate job discrimination against these women or their spouses as plausible explanations. Their analysis of the impact of local labor market conditions on the labor force participation of married women controls for five variables: unemployment, female earnings, industry mix, supply of females, and wages of domestics. Cross-sectional regressions for Standard Metropolitan Statistical Areas (SMSAs) yielded intercity comparisons. Market discrimination was and still is a variable that is hard to quantify.

Because Bowen and Finegan combined several widely different groups into the category of single women, their labor force participation rates for this group do not match the Current Population Survey (CPS) and other census classifications. They defined "single women" to be those in urban areas who were "*not* married with husband present." This group included women who were never married as well as women who were widowed, divorced, separated, and married with spouse absent. The greater financial pressure on some of these women may not warrant the aggregation of these groups.

Bowen and Finegan also treated the labor force participation rates of these single women as a function of color, other income, schooling, and age. The black-white differential in the labor force participation rates of all single women was 7 percentage points higher for whites in the unadjusted rates, but these differences disappeared after the influence of other income, marital status, schooling, and age were taken into account. The authors concluded that the overall nonsignificance of color in the single women regression is evidence "that a number of important forces associated with this variable, pulling in opposite directions, have struggled to a tie."[10]

Young black women workers both in and out of school in urban areas had significantly lower labor force participation rates than young white women. Even when these labor force participation rates were adjusted for a number of variables, including age, other family income, family size, family status, schooling of family head, and labor force status of the family head, these rates were substantially lower for blacks in 1960.[11] The exceedingly unfavorable labor market position of black teenage females is discussed in chapter 6.

Bell

Duran Bell stated in "Why Participation Rates of Black and White Wives Differ," that factors that induce market work among black wives are fundamentally different from those affecting white wives. He used data from the 1967 Survey of Economic Opportunity (SEO) to examine the extent to which black and white wives have different labor force responses to specified variables; the extent to which the differences in the labor force participation of black and white wives may be explained by the differences in family and personal characteristics as opposed to different responses to given characteristics; and the factors underlying the differences in response.[12] Bell tested the impact of age, education, geographic region, other family income, number of children, children under the age of four, residential location, number of weeks during 1966 that the husband did not work, and previous marriage on labor force participation of black and white wives. The difference in the participation rates for black and white wives who worked full-time in 1966 was large—45.9 percent versus 32.9 percent. Black wives had almost 40 percent higher labor force participation than white wives.

Bell argued that the differences in the participation rates of black and white women seem to reflect differences in black responses to the specified variables. In addition, Bell stated that "Cain and Bowen and Finegan explain the higher labor force participation of black wives in terms of factors which are no longer appropriate: (1) the greater prevalence of part-time work among black wives, and (2) the poorer housing conditions facing black families, which induce the doubling up of families within a given residence and improve the availability of child care."[13]

In contrast to Cain and Bowen and Finegan, Bell showed that "black families in which the wife works full-time are among the more stable and better educated families, where-as the white working wife emerges from the lesser educated, poorer, and more unstable white families . . . Black wives who do not work represent an impoverished class which is signifi-cant within the black population but rather small within the white population . . . White wives who do not work represent an enriched class which is significant among white but not among black families."[14] Moreover, Bell differs from Cain in stating that "While the black mother may have somewhat better access to relatives for child care purposes, the long-term inadequacy of the black husband's earnings is clearly a factor which influences not only the effect of children upon LFP but the entire lifetime pattern of his wife's economic activity."[15]

Bell believes that his results differ significantly from those of the earlier researchers because of the dramatic changes in the opportunities for blacks. He speculated that future stud-ies of black/white differences in labor force participation using 1970 data would likely show the same kinds of dif-ferences as his study. However, the strong increase in the labor force participation of white wives since 1970 has reduced the differential.

National Longitudinal Surveys

One of the most detailed studies of labor market experience

is the National Longitudinal Surveys (NLS) of women who were 30 to 44 years old in 1967. (The Center for Human Resource Research at The Ohio State University also undertook surveys for three other age-sex cohorts, older men 45 to 59 years old and young men and women 14 to 24 years old.) A national probability sample of this cohort group of women from the noninstitutional population has been periodically interviewed now for almost ten years. Four volumes of reports entitled *Dual Careers* cover the first five years of the study, 1967-1972. In order to permit a more confident analysis of differences in the labor market experience of blacks and whites, blacks were substantially overrepresented in the sample; of a sample of 5,083 individuals 1,390 were black. A detailed work history of the respondents as well as information on social, psychological, and economic characteristics that affect labor market activity were included.

The National Longitudinal Surveys data showed that although black women were less well prepared than white women (by their education, training, and personal characteristics) for the world of work, these black women had more pressures inducing them to enter the labor market. Black wives were more likely to have husbands who were either unable to work at all or who were employed less than fulltime during the year. More than twice as many black women as white women lived in households with other family members in which total annual income, exclusive of their own earnings, was under $3,000.[16]

The NLS data were used to analyze three dimensions of labor force participation for these mature women: current participation; lifetime participation, based on their total history since leaving school; and prospective activity, based on response to questions about their future plans. The findings of the NLS study were consistent with other research on the influence of marital status, presence and ages of children, level of education, and husband's earnings on the labor force participation of women. The NLS data also confirmed the existence of pronounced differences in the extent of labor market activity between white and black women. By all measures of current, past, and prospective participation black women had higher participation rates than white women in the initial year of the study, and the differences did not appear to be completely accounted for by the intercolor differences in the tested variables.[17]

The NLS data (1967–1972) showed a large increase in labor force participation for white women and a decrease for black women as the cohorts aged over the five-year period. The white participation rate rose by about 9 points, while the black participation rate dropped by 4 points. Thus the 20 point black/white differential at the beginning of the period was reduced by almost two-thirds by 1972. The trend of labor force participation among whites was dominated by women with children. The NLS data, however, show a more pronounced racial convergence in the labor force participation rates than comparable data from the Current Population Survey.[18] A sobering conclusion from the NLS study is that in "virtually every respect that has been examined by the studies in this volume, black women fare less well than white women. One expects to find *gross* racial differentials, of course, as a result of the disadvantage of blacks in the characteristics (for example, education) that affect labor market position. But the inferior labor market position of black women persists even when these factors are controlled as fully as possible with the data at hand."[19]

Jones

The NLS panel data have been made available to other researchers, and a number of studies have been conducted on the mature women cohorts. Barbara Jones, in *The Contribution of Black Women to the Incomes of Black Families*, examined the labor force participation of black wives with spouse present (945 in the NLS sample) in order to determine the impact of the wives' earnings on the incomes of black families. In addition to the usual personal and economic variables that are related to labor force participation of wives, Jones also tested the employment history of the wife, family

assets, health of wife, presence of other adults in the household, cost of child care and transportation, geographic
mobility patterns, and size of the hometown. Calculation of
adjusted participation rates for black wives was done by
controlling for the most powerful variables: wife's earnings,
wife's health, other family income, and number of family
members. Her major findings were generally consistent with
other studies, with three exceptions. More schooling (with
earnings held constant) has a negative influence on the
decision of black wives to work. Contrary to Cain's findings,
the age of the children influences work decisions: small
children exert a negative force and older children exert a
positive force. Jones's study differs from Bell's because indebtedness is not significant in determining labor force
participation of black wives.[20]

Summary

These have been the major economic studies of the labor
force participation of black women, especially those women
who are married with spouse present. Not only do these
studies use different analytical approaches to the labor force
participation trends of black women but there is no consensus on the facts. Cain noted that although the levels of
labor force participation of black wives were higher, the rate
of increase over time was slower than for white wives. Bowen
and Finegan concluded that perhaps the effect of color per se
on the labor force participation of black women had been
exaggerated. Bell was critical of the studies by Cain and
Bowen and Finegan and identified the long-term inadequacy
of the earnings of black husbands as a significant factor in
the labor force behavior of black wives. The data from the
National Longitudinal Survey confirmed the reduction in the
labor force participation of black and white women. Jones's
findings were generally consistent with the other studies,
except that she found that schooling has a negative influence
on the decision of black wives to work; contrary to Cain's
findings, the age of children does influence the decision to

work; and contrary to Bell's results, indebtedness is not significant in determining the labor force participation of black wives.

We still do not understand fully why the labor force participation of black wives has become weaker than that for white women. Perhaps the models of joint participation rates by husbands and wives used in determining family labor supply may eventually provide some insight on this issue.[21] In a theoretical vein, Loury has persuasively argued for the significance of social forces outside an individual's control that determine the acquisition of standard human capital characteristics. He notes that it is unlikely that analysis of these forces will develop within the confines of traditional neoclassical economic theory.[22]

3

---

*Selected Supply
Characteristics of Black
Women Workers*

In this chapter the labor market activity of black women is reviewed in terms of occupational status, work schedules (part time and full time), educational attainment, and presence of children. These characteristics demonstrate significant differences between black women workers and their white counterparts. The statistics presented in this chapter are from a variety of government documents, which merely provide a snapshot at a given moment. The data have not been adjusted for overall changes in the structure of the economy. Nevertheless, several paradoxes emerge from the data.

Many studies have emphasized the convergence in the occupational position of black and white women since 1960, and others have focused on the relative disparity of the occupational status of black women over the span of their careers. Despite considerable upgrading of the occupational status of black women, they remain "crowded" into public sector jobs while white women work mainly in private sector jobs. One bright spot has been the shift from part-time to full-time work during the 1960–1970 decade and the presumed improvement in the economic status of black women workers.

Occupational Status

Although black women workers have made significant gains in upgrading their occupational status, they are still more likely than whites to be in blue-collar and service positions. In June 1978 the proportion of white women in white-collar occupations was almost one and one-half times as high as that of black women (65.3 percent versus 45.5 percent).

Between 1965 and 1978, however, the percentage of black women in white-collar jobs nearly doubled and the percentage in service occupations, including private household jobs, declined by nearly 40 percent. (See table 3.1.)

Black employment increased by 52 percent between 1960 and 1978, and black women accounted for about 60 percent of that increase. The cross-sectional data from the 1970 census show several major shifts from the 1960 occupational positions for black women. In 1960 about 34 percent of all black employed women were private household workers; by 1970 that proportion had declined to 14 percent. Clerical workers represented 8.4 of employed black women in 1960 and 19.4 percent in 1970. (See table R.5.)

Bell and Freeman examined the process of occupational change and concluded that the major factor producing convergence in black and white female job structures was the great difference between cohorts entering and leaving the labor force. By 1970 three-fifths of the black women who were household workers were over 45 years of age, and 72 percent of all household workers resided in the South. Young black women found employment in other occupations. Their improved options were associated with both educational attainment and operation of antidiscrimination laws.[1]

Bell attributed much of the improved relative economic position of black women to their "reallocation among occupations." Twenty-five percent of the black women entering the labor force were clerical workers compared with only 3 percent of the retiring black women in that occupation. "At the same time, 53 percent of the retiring black female workers had been private household workers while only 8 percent of the entering black women accepted that occupation. Hence, there was a dramatic switch from domestic to clerical work for black women."[2]

Fifteen percent of the new entrants among black women were professional and technical workers compared with 6 percent of the retiring black women in this group. Seven and a half percent of employed black women were professional and technical workers in 1960 compared with 11 percent in

Table 3.1 Women in Major Occupation Groups, 1965 and 1978

Occupation	1965 Black	White	1978 Black	White
White-collar workers	23.5%	60.2%	45.5%	65.3%
Blue-collar workers	15.8	16.3	20.1	14.2
Service workers	54.6	19.8	33.4	19.1
Farm workers	6.1	3.6	1.9	1.4

Sources: *Employment and Earnings,* vol. 11, no. 12 (May 1965): A-21; and *Employment and Earnings,* vol. 25, no. 6 (June 1978): A-22.

1970. In 1970, however, teachers (except college and university teachers) and registered nurses accounted for about 62 percent of black women professional and technical workers in the experienced civilian labor force.* (See tables 3.2, R.6, and R.7 for black-white detailed occupational comparisons in 1970.)

Although the percentage of employed black women who were clerical workers more than doubled between 1960 and 1970, most of these women were at the bottom of the hierarchy and did not work in the private sector. As late as 1976 Malvoaux found that black women were at the bottom of the hierarchy in more than three-quarters of the forty-four detailed occupations in the Survey of Income and Education.[3] Almost two-fifths of black women clerical workers held government jobs, and another 10 percent were employed in nonprofit organizations. The National Longitudinal Survey data showed that although the proportions of white women employed in clerical occupations by government and nongovernment employers were similar, only 10 percent of the black wage and salary workers employed in the private sector were in clerical occupations compared to 32 percent employed by the government.[4]

The National Longitudinal Survey investigated the determinants of the occupational status of women in their first jobs

*The experienced civilian labor force comprises employed and unemployed persons who have worked at any time in the past.

Table 3.2 Selected Black Women Professional Workers in the
Experienced Civilian Labor Force, 1970

Occupation	Number	Percentage of Total	Median Years of School
Teachers, except college and university	177,240	45	16.5
Registered nurses	62,799	16	12.7
Total professional and technical workers	388,960	100.0	16.0

Source: U.S. Department of Commerce, Bureau of the Census.
Census of Population: 1970. Final Report PC (2)-7A, *Occupational
Characteristics.* See table R.6.

after the completion of their education. A survey of mature
women (30–44 years old) taken in 1967 and 1972 determined
that the status of their first jobs was associated with race even
after education and other explanatory variables (age, marital
and family status, education of parents, occupation of head
of household when respondent was 15 years old) were
introduced. This evidence was consistent with the fact that
labor market discrimination existed prior to the 1960s, when
the respondents were leaving school.[5]

The occupational status of black women relative to white
women deteriorated over the period between their first jobs
and the survey in 1967, and this trend in the racial differential
appears to have continued over the five-year period from
1967 to 1972. Thus black women in their thirties and forties
who were employed in both 1967 and 1972 did not fare as
well relative to whites as cross-sectional data for the entire
labor force would suggest.[6] Parnes and Nestel noted that
even after controlling for all other factors, the relative disparity of the occupational status of black women still widened
during the time they were in the labor force. "This is an
additional reminder that the rather impressive effort in recent
years in combatting racial discrimination in the labor market
still leaves something to be desired."[7]

Selected Supply Characteristics of Black Women Workers

Finally, Garfinkle, using data from the annual Current Population Survey (CPS) has traced the occupational participation* of black women from 1962 to 1974. (See table R.8.) The major finding of this study is that black women, relative to their white counterparts, made more pervasive inroads into the high-paying occupations than black men; that is, black women vis-a-vis white women did better than black males vis-a-vis white males.[8] The favorable occupational comparisons of black women with white women merely highlights the inferior occupational status of most women regardless of color. Black women *relative* to all others in the labor market have not made the spectacular gains often cited in popular journals. (See table R.9.)

Work Schedules

An alternative measure of market work is the amount of labor supplied in number of hours worked annually. Labor participation rates include both full- and part-time workers, and these numbers may obscure the intensity of the work effort. Both Cain and Bowen and Finegan concluded that because black women workers were less likely to have full-time jobs, labor force participation had to be adjusted accordingly. However, one of the significant changes beginning in the late 1960s was the shift away from part-time to full-time employment by black women. A study by the U.S. Bureau of Labor Statistics reported that "About 22 percent of the working white adult women in 1977 had voluntary part-time jobs, compared with 15 percent of the blacks." This study also noted that ". . . [W]hite women, more often than black women, choose to work part-time when financial need does not require full-time work. Important reasons for their working part time may include upgrading or maintaining job skill or enjoying the nonpecuniary benefits of employment."[9]

---

*Ratio of a particular group employed in an occupation relative to all workers in that occupation.

The official definitions of part-time and full-time work are not uniform. The definition used in the Current Population Survey (CPS) conducted monthly for the Bureau of Labor Statistics encompasses voluntary and involuntary part-time employment as well as full-time schedules. The Bureau of Labor Statistics publishes an annual special report on "Work Experience of the Population," compiled from supplementary questions to the March CPS, which shows the number of individuals who worked during the year and the number employed by age, race, sex, and marital and household status. In these reports part-time work is less than 35 hours per week, and full-time work is 35 hours or more per week. Year-round full-time work is full-time work for 50 to 52 weeks, and part-year work is full- or part-time work for 1 to 49 weeks. Thus primary and secondary school teachers who work 9 to 10 months a year on a full-time basis would be classified as part-year workers, and part-time employment would include both year-round and part-year work. (See tables R.10 and R.11.)

Although the proportion of black women in voluntary part-time employment has declined during the past decade, the profile of black women in this category contrasts sharply with that of white women. Bell found that black married women who worked part time were less educated, had less-educated husbands, and less other family income than those who worked full time. The reverse tended to be true for white wives.[10] The NLS studies on mature women workers show that married white women who worked part time were from families in which the median income was higher than for those who worked full time. The relationship was reversed for married black women.[11]

A higher proportion of white women who work part time are classified as voluntary part-time workers or individuals desiring less than full-time work. Black women, on the other hand, state economic reasons for their part-time work. Economic reasons include slack work, material shortages, plant or equipment repair, inability to find full-time work. In 1977, 31 percent of black women and 16 percent of white women

Selected Supply Characteristics of Black Women Workers

working on part-time schedules were doing so involuntarily (for economic reasons). Statistics on the full-time labor force and part-time labor force tell another interesting story.* During the period 1968–1977 the number of black women increased 45 percent in the full-time labor force and 16 percent in the part-time labor force compared with 34 percent and 45 percent, respectively, for white women workers. About 8 percent of the black women in the full-time labor force and about 5 percent of the white women in the full-time labor force worked involuntarily on a part-time basis. (See tables 3.3 and 3.4.) The shift of black women to full-time work may have been due to the reduction of barriers in labor markets, reflected in occupational upgrading, improvement in educational attainment, and greater economic pressure to contribute to family income. In recent years all of these factors have interacted to produce greater labor force participation of married black women, even as the incomes of their husbands increased.

Educational Attainment

In the various economic models of labor force participation of women, education is a powerful explanatory variable. Although education has been Identified as one of the most important factors in reducing the earnings gap between black and white women workers, there is still much debate about some of the comparisons. The median number of years of schooling for black women in the labor force increased from 8.1 in 1952 to 12.4 in 1975 compared with 12.1 and 12.6 years in 1952 and 1975, respectively, for white women workers. The significant reduction in the educational gap surely accounts for some of the relative income gain. The median number of

*The full-time labor force consists of persons employed full time, persons employed part time for economic reasons, and unemployed persons seeking full-time work. The part-time labor force consists of persons voluntarily employed part time and unemployed persons seeking part-time work.

Table 3.3 Women in the Part-Time Labor Force, 1968–1977
(× 1000)

Year	Total	Employed Part-Time	Unemployed	
			Number	Percentage
1968				
Black women	755	683	71	9.5
White women	6,027	5,716	312	5.2
1969				
Black women	785	720	65	8.3
White women	6,372	6,050	322	5.1
1970				
Black women	788	709	79	10.0
White women	6,824	6,421	403	5.9
1971				
Black women	794	702	92	11.6
White women	7,021	6,538	482	6.9
1972				
Black women	822	723	99	12.1
White women	7,317	6,831	486	6.6
1973				
Black women	839	740	99	11.8
White women	7,661	7,184	477	6.2
1974				
Black women	826	733	93	11.3
White women	7,929	7,372	557	7.0
1975				
Black women	876	748	129	14.7
White women	8,081	7,400	681	8.4
1976				
Black women	867	719	128	15.1
White women	8,457	7,777	679	8.0
1977				
Black women	878	736	142	16.1
White women	8,772	8,078	694	7.9

Source: U.S. Department of Labor, Bureau of Labor Statistics, unpublished data.

Table 3.4 Women in the Full-Time Labor Force, 1968–1977
(× 1,000)

Year	Total	Employed Full-Time	Employed Part-Time for Economic Reasons	Unemployment Number	Percentage
1968					
Black women	3,026	2,534	250	242	8.0
White women	19,396	17,938	686	772	4.0
1969					
Black women	3,133	2,660	234	239	7.6
White women	20,222	18,674	746	802	4.0
1970					
Black women	3,277	2,659	274	294	9.1
White women	20,681	18,731	873	1,078	5.2
1971					
Black women	3,308	2,682	273	353	10.7
White women	20,968	18,665	1,014	1,290	6.2
1972					
Black women	3,427	2,777	267	382	11.2
White women	21,712	19,451	1,022	1,238	5.7
1973					
Black women	3,631	3,026	232	372	10.3
White women	22,380	20,237	1,027	1,116	5.0
1974					
Black women	3,807	3,120	284	404	10.6
White women	23,262	20,743	1,165	1,354	5.8
1975					
Black women	3,918	3,029	347	542	13.8
White women	24,122	20,568	1,460	2,093	8.7
1976					
Black women	4,197	3,311	326	560	13.3
White women	24,914	21,534	1,427	1,953	7.8
1977					
Black women	4,388	3,466	327	595	13.6
White women	25,914	22,530	1,498	1,336	7.1

Source: U.S. Department of Labor, Bureau of Labor Statistics, unpublished data.

years of school completed by occupational categories ranged from 9.2 for private household service workers to 16.4 for professional and managerial workers. (See table R.12.) However, the median number of years of school completed by black women who worked as clericals and salespersons has ranged from 12.5 to 12.7 grades since mid-1952. The educational attainment of this group was almost the same as for white women, yet the massive shift of black women workers into this occupation, from 9 percent of all black women workers in 1960 to slightly less than 20 percent in 1970, did not occur until the latter part of the 1960s. Was this occupational upgrading induced by easing of discrimination barriers, change in the structure of urban labor markets and the movement of some jobs out of cities, manpower programs, and factors other than educational attainment?

Bowen and Finegan argue that additional years of schooling increase a women's expected market earnings and thus encourage her to substitute time in the labor market for work at home. "Years of school completed may serve as a proxy for underlying tastes for market work and for natural aptitudes for employment."[12] Their empirical findings show strong positive association between schooling (when allowance is made for color, presence of children, age, other family income and employment status of husband) and labor force participation of married women.

Black married women constitute the important exception to the tendency for the adjusted participation rates to increase regularly with educational attainment. However, the adjusted participation rate for black women with 16 or more years of school completed is extraordinarily high—83 percent. The authors concluded that black women who are college graduates are a highly selective group and many professional opportunities are open to them. The authors also explain, in part, the apparently weaker association between education and earnings opportunities for black women who are *not* college graduates in terms of a less favorable differential gain in access to more desirable jobs. Because the participation rate of married women is affected by access to more interesting jobs (psychic income) as well as pay, one expects large increases in the percentage of women who fill the more desirable jobs as the educational level shifts from elementary school or less to high school graduate.[13] My hypothesis of the 1960 behavior of the schooling-specific participation profile of black married women with 0–12 years of school completed is that barriers in the labor market prevented black women with the same educational attainment as white women from gaining access to the more desirable occupations.

What at first seems to be a contrary finding by Jones, that additional schooling discourages the labor force participation of black wives, may also be consistent with the hypothesis that difficulties in labor markets discourage their labor force participation. Bowen and Finegan concluded that as schooling increased, both wage and nonwage effects were associated with changes in the labor force participation rate of white wives. Thus for wives with more than 17 years of schooling, about 65 percent of the increase in labor force participation was attributed to nonwage effects, such as better hours, interesting work, and opportunities for promotion.[14] Jones speculated that the same nonwage advantages were not available to both well-educated white women and black wives.[15] This explains why her adjusted labor force participation rate for black wives (controlled for health, number of family members, other family incomes, and earnings or potential earnings) who have attained 5 or more years of college is lower than for those who have less schooling.

Gurin and Gaylord questioned the validity of two premises: (1) highly educated professional black women enjoy a favored position in the labor market, and (2) these women possess unusual motivational strengths in the world of work. They found that black women face wage discrimination by race and do no better than black males in the labor market.[16] Of course, the differential between the median earnings of full-time black and white women workers, when controlled for education and number of weeks worked, may derive from other types of discrimination (occupational, access to human capital after schooling, and employment). In contrast to the conventional wisdom, Gurin and Gaylord showed that black college women do not possess unusual motivational strengths. Their recent research on the occupational and educational aspiration of several thousand students attending predominately black schools demonstrated that women seniors in colleges differ significantly from men in educational expectations; black college women tend to aspire to occupations that have less prestige, require less ability, and are less subject to racial discrimination than black college men; and black women aspire to a smaller range of jobs but do not differ substantially from men in terms of motives, values, and self-confidence according to standard psychological tests.[17]

While the economic models of labor force participation of women have introduced education of women as an explanatory variable, sociologists have associated the occupational status and income of an individual with the education and occupation of the parent (family head). Moreover, because of differences in the quality of schooling received by black children, the offspring of a black family of the same size and socioeconomic standing as a white family may earn less income than the offspring of a white family. To the extent that the quality of education that an individual receives influences his later income, the black child will be at a disadvantage. Although these sociological studies have been focused mainly on the male population, it is likely that black women have similar experiences.[18]

Age and Presence of Children

Although the presence of children typically places a strong constraint on labor force participation of mothers, there have always been differences in the responses of black and white women with children. In the past, white women tended to stay out of the labor force during their childbearing and child rearing years, and black married women, regardless of their education, worked continuously. Recently, however,

there has been a significant increase in labor force participation among white wives (spouses present) with small
children, and a larger number of divorced and separated
women with children are now working. Even so, black working wives with young children devote more time to paid work
than white wives. However, black female heads of families,
especially never-married young women with children under
six, have lower labor force participation rates than other
women.

Bowen and Finegan and Cain noted that the net effect of
children on the labor force participation of married women
varied in accordance with the ages and number of children
and as a result of interaction with other variables. For 1960
they found that the presence of children under 14 years of
age, and especially children under 6 years of age, discouraged labor force participation of white married women.
The presence of older children (14–17 years old) apparently
encouraged mothers of young children to enter the labor
force by providing assistance with home tasks.[19] Black wives,
however, (after controlling for age, schooling, other family
income, and employment status of the husband) tended to
have higher participation rates even when their children were
under 6 years of age. Jones also found that the participation
rates for mature black wives* with preschool-age children
was lower than those for wives without preschool children.[20]

Within the past decade government labor force participation statistics of working mothers have focused on wives as
well as other women who head families. The differences in
the economic situation between the two types of families are
large. Of the 60.6 million own children**under 18 years of age
as of March 1977, 48 percent had mothers in the work force.

---

*Beginning with the initial interviews of mid-1967, the National
Longitudinal Survey and other studies based on these data refer to
mature women as those 30 to 44 years of age.

**Own children are sons and daughters, including stepchildren and
adopted children, of the family head.

The 28.9 million children of working mothers included 6.4 million children under six years of age. Of the 7.9 million black children under 18 years of age, approximately 55 percent had working mothers compared with 46 percent of white children who had working mothers. (See Table 3.5.) The type of family represented by the black and white working mothers differed. Children of white working mothers were overwhelmingly situated (85 percent) in husband-wife families, with a median income of $17,588, and 42 percent of the children of black working mothers in 1975 from female-headed families with a median income of $5,752.

The current controversy over why the presence of preschool children apparently does not have the same effect on black working mothers who are heads of families as it does for other working mothers is an issue that is beyond the scope of this study. The paramount social issue is the welfare of black children, and an expeditious move toward the resolution of this problem may not preclude but rather complement programs to improve the employment status of poor black women. In 1976 more than half of all black children were in families in which the father was absent, unemployed, or not in the labor force.[21]

Summary

Economic studies on the determinants of labor force participation of women, especially those who are married with spouse present, have indentified a large number of personal, family, and economic explanatory variables. Four variables—occupational status, work schedules, educational attainment, and age and presence of children—account for differences between black and white women workers. Perhaps the most noticeable difference was the impact of the presence of small children on the work efforts of wives. Certainly the increased labor force participation of white mothers with small children will elevate the provision of extrafamily child care to a national issue.[22]

Table 3.5 Presence of Children by Family Type and Labor Force Status of Mother March 1977 (× 1,000)

Type of Family	Children Under 18 Years	Children Under 6 Years	Children Under 18 Years with Mothers in Labor Force	Children Under 6 Years with Mothers in Labor Force
Total[a]	60,584	17,117	28,892	6,431
Black	7,905	2,144	4,360	1,062
White	51,500	14,574	23,915	5,191
Husband/wife[a]	50,279	14,780	23,341	5,411
Black	4,318	1,205	2,597	694
White	44,932	13,208	20,206	4,553
Female Head[a]	9,499	2,233	5,551	1,020
Black	3,482	913	1,763	368
White	5,878	1,288	3,710	639
Male Head[a]	807	104		
Black	106	26		
White	690	78		

Source: Allyson Sherman Grossman, "Children of Working Mothers, March 1977," *Monthly Labor Review*, January 1978.

a. Includes other races not shown.

4

Labor Market Policies

A key factor in understanding the labor force participation of black women is the structure of the labor markets. The concentration of a disproportionate number of these workers in secondary labor markets—jobs with low pay, high turnover, and limited opportunities for advancement—discourages participation. Competing theoretical explanations have been offered for the labor market difficulties of black women. Human capital models focus on the personal characteristics of individuals, and dual or segmented labor market theorists emphasize the "characteristics of jobs and job markets."

Human capital theory posits that differential earnings of women are a function of their productivity attributes, such as education, skill level, or work experience. Its perspective is almost exclusively technologically determined. The human capital approach was implicitly incorporated into the framework of most of the manpower programs of the 1960s. It was believed that workers who entered the labor market with deficient skills and education and other handicaps could be made more attractive to employers through training and development programs, which would increase annual earnings and improve the labor force participation of these workers.

Dual labor market proponents perceive the labor market to be segmented into a primary sector and a secondary sector. The primary sector is characterized by jobs with "high wages, good working conditions, employment stability, chances of advancement and equity and due process in the administration of work rules."[1] Workers with high levels of skills and knowledge are involved with advanced technologies. The wags of individual workers in the primary sector are determined by the workings of the highly structured internal labor market with the mechanism of external labor markets operating at a distance.[2] The secondary sector, on the other hand, consists of low-paying jobs with considerable instability, poor working conditions, and less systematic and equitable administration of work rules. The primary and secondary labor markets are vastly different. "Workers with particular ascriptive traits (such as age, race, and sex) will not be distributed evenly among the different job clusters . . . Labor mobility tends to be greater within than between segments."[3] Whether a strict dichotomy between the primary and secondary markets prevails, there are limitations for the less favored workers, such as black women, even in the primary sector. The primary sector is subdivided into upper- and lower-tier jobs. The upper-tier jobs include professional and managerial jobs, which are distinguished by higher pay and status, greater promotion opportunities, more emphasis on education as a screening device, and greater latitude for individual creativity and initiative. The lower-tier jobs in the primary sector consist of mainly well-paying blue-collar jobs.

Discrimination is the major institutional barrier that confines certain workers to secondary labor markets. The conventional economic definition of employment discrimination is that workers of the same ability receive differential earnings. Becker's neoclassical model of utility maximization traced the consequences of a "taste for discrimination" by employers, employees, and consumers. Discrimination coefficients that correspond to tariffs in international trade measure the monetary premium paid by different individuals or groups for not associating with blacks, women, or other groups.[4] There have been some criticisms of this model and there have been attempts to remedy deficiencies. One leading neoclassical economist recently noted that "The large and *persisting* differentials in earnings between white and black males and between males and females—even when productivity indicators are apparently equal—do indeed challenge orthodox theory."[5]

An alternative concept to the "central" neoclassical model is based on employers' "perception of reality." Statistical discrimination posits that when an employer incurs some costs in order to determine a potential employee's true productivity, the employer assesses the prospective employee on the basis of preconsidered ideas of the average characteristics of the group or groups to which the applicant belongs rather than the individual's characteristics. The sizeable body of empirical studies on employment discrimination that has been produced by economists during the past decade further reflects a theoretical split. Some support has been found for human capital models and some for the dual labor market theories.

This chapter is devoted mainly to a discussion of how three labor market conditions, employment and training programs, unemployment, and employment discrimination, affect the labor force behavior of black women. Two other structural factors, public sector employment and unionism, are examined also in order to determine the impact on the relative economic status of black women.

Employment and Training Programs

The employment and training programs of the past seventeen years have been designed to enable the federal government to assist in augmenting the human capital of disadvantaged, unemployed, and underemployed individuals. A variety of skill training, job development, work experience, and employability development programs was supported under the Manpower Development and Training Act (MDTA) of 1962, as amended, and the Economic Opportunity Act of 1964. Many of the categorical programs have been administered since 1973 by state and local government agencies under the Comprehensive Employment and Training Act (CETA), which superseded MDTA.

In an exhaustive study of the impact of government manpower programs on the position of women and minority workers, Perry and his colleagues at the Wharton School concluded that "black women were among the major recipients of manpower services."[6] They examined the data from a large number of evaluative studies on program impact and detailed information for the operating statistics of different manpower programs. Unfortunately, much of the statistical data from the evaluative studies does not show minorities disaggregated into male and female categories. Statistics from program operations for the fiscal years 1965 through 1972 show that 46.3 percent of first-time enrollees in major manpower programs were black and 43.9 percent were women. Both groups were overwhelmingly enrolled in programs that emphasized neither skill training nor job development.

Did participation in these employment and training programs increase the level and quality of labor force participation of black women as measured by occupational ungrading, higher earnings, an greater employment stability? Black women were disproportionately concentrated in programs that did not provide skill training and did little to broaden their job horizons. Even when they enrolled in skill-training programs under MDTA, they were forced into two narrow occupational fields: health and clerical occupations.[7] Perry et al. concluded from the evaluative studies (sample data collected by researchers) of manpower programs that participants, including black women, experienced higher average annual earnings in the immediate post-program period than just prior to their participation and their differentials on earnings, wages, and employment were narrowed.[8]

The Perry study noted that evidence from the program operating statistics showed that both blacks and women experienced larger gains in their post-training levels than did white males. Although black women in the Concentrated Employment Program (CEP), Work Incentive Program (WIN), and the Job Corps made the largest relative gains, they still had the lowest post-training earnings among the four race-sex groups in these programs.[9]

It has been difficult to measure the economic benefits of employment and training programs because most of the evaluative studies did not have comparison groups. Perhaps one of the best sources of information for program evaluation is the one percent Continuous Work History Sample of the

Social Security Administration. These longitudinal series on individual earnings have information for almost the entire labor force by race, sex, geographic region, and industry. Nicholas Kiefer has estimated the effect of training in four major manpower programs—MDTA/Institutional Training, JOBS, Job Corps, and Neighborhood Youth Corps out-of-school component—based on earnings, employment, and labor force participation.[10] Kiefer has linked the Office of Economic Opportunity/Department of Labor longitudinal manpower data set with annual earnings records from the Social Security Administration. Kiefer calculated mean annual earnings of trainees and controls from the Social Security Administration data base for the period 1965–1973. Training in these programs occurred in 1969.

The mean quarterly earnings for the three quarters before training and the three quarters after training showed that adult black women in the MDTA and JOBS programs earned more, on the average, than women in the comparison group. For example, black women in the MDTA and JOBS programs had mean quarterly earnings of $615 and $432, respectively, in the third quarter after training compared with $264 for the comparison group. (Part of the earnings difference was due to the fact that the trainees worked more weeks and were paid a higher rate.) Despite the apparent increase in earnings of black women in these training programs, the largest increases in earnings, employment, and participation occurred for "nonblack females" in the JOBS program.[11]

An enormous amount of information is now being collected in order to assess the impact of the several titles of the CETA programs. Although the intended focus of these programs was to be on the structurally unemployed workers, the 1974–1975 recession shifted the emphasis to temporary countercyclical public service jobs that were held by better educated nonminority group males. Recently employment and training programs have been targeted once more on disadvantaged individuals, and black women greatly in need of skill training as well as work experience may benefit.[12] Large sums have been spent by the federal government to improve the potential productivity of "disadvantaged" individuals, but it has been difficult to document significant *permanent* gains for black women from their participation in these employment and training programs.

Unemployment

Unemployment is far from a random phenomenon. It tends to plague certain categories of individuals from one year to another. Since World War II black workers have borne a disproportionate share of the burden. The frequent interruption of the work experience of blacks has been attributed to their concentration in occupations were unemployment tends to be high, entrapment in secondary labor markets with low wages and unattractive working conditions, poor health records, educational and skill deficiencies, and employment discrimination.

Throughout the post-war period the unemployment rates for black women have been higher than those for white women—in some years they were at least double. (See table 4.1.) Black female teenagers have experienced sharply higher unemployment rates, and black female heads of families, with their unfavorable labor market status, have accounted for a large share of black unemployment. For other black adult women, high rates of unemployment may be subject to the vagaries of the business cycle. In March 1978 black women experienced an unemployment rate of 13.6 percent compared to 6.0 percent for white women. The highest rates were experienced by black single women (23.4 percent), which includes the teenage component. (See table 4.2.)

In addition to the unemployment statistics, the Bureau of Labor Statistics now regularly reports on the "discouraged" workers, workers with low expectations for finding a job who, after long periods of unemployment, withdraw from the labor force. A more recent statistic has been the jobless rate (difference between the potential labor force and the actual

Table 4.1 Unemployment Rates for Women by Color, 1948–1978

Year	Black	White	Black/White Ratio
1948	6.1	3.8	1.61
1949	7.9	5.7	1.39
1950	8.4	5.3	1.58
1951	6.1	4.2	1.45
1952	5.7	3.3	1.73
1953	4.1	3.1	1.32
1954	9.3	5.6	1.66
1955	8.4	4.3	1.95
1956	8.9	4.2	2.12
1957	7.3	4.3	1.70
1958	10.8	6.2	1.74
1959	9.4	5.3	1.77
1960	9.4	5.3	1.77
1961	11.8	6.5	1.82
1962	11.0	5.5	2.00
1963	11.2	5.8	1.93
1964	10.6	5.5	1.93
1965	9.2	5.0	1.84
1966	8.6	4.3	2.00
1967	9.1	4.6	1.98
1968	8.3	4.3	1.93
1969	7.8	4.2	1.86
1970	9.3	5.4	1.72
1971	10.8	6.3	1.71
1972	11.3	5.9	1.92
1973	10.5	5.3	1.98
1974	10.7	6.1	1.75
1975	14.0	8.6	1.63
1976	13.6	7.9	1.72
1977	14.0	7.3	1.92
1978	13.1	6.2	2.11

Source: U.S. Department of Labor, Employment and Training Administration, *Employment and Training Report of the President,* 1979, Table A-27.

Labor Market Policies

Table 4.2 Unemployment Rates for Women By Marital Status, March 1978

Marital Status	Black	White	Black/White Ratio
Si ̇gle	23.4	8.9	2.63
Married			
spouse present	8.1	4.8	1.69
spouse absent	14.8	8.7	1.70
Widowed	8.8	4.3	2.05
Divorced	8.1	6.3	1.29
Total	13.6	6.0	2.27

Source: U.S. Department of Labor, Bureau of Labor Statistics, *Marital and Family Characteristics*, March 1978.

employment).* Black workers have been a sizeable part of that pool of people just beyond the boundary of the labor market. In 1975, 66 percent of the black women who left the unemployed category actually left the labor force and 33 percent found jobs. By comparison, 45 percent of the white women who left unemployment found jobs.[13]

Gilroy analyzed the unemployment burden of blacks when the demand for labor changes. Conventional wisdom was that the unemployment situation of blacks deteriorates compared with that of whites in the downswing of the business cycle and improves on the upswing. Gilroy concluded that the differing cyclical unemployment experience of blacks has been mitigated over recent business cycles. However, over the long period, in recovery and downturn, blacks still are affected relatively more than whites by changes in the demand for labor.[14]

The greater cyclical sensitivity of black workers has been investigated by several researchers who have designed job search-turnover models of the labor market by age, race, and sex categories. Barrett and Morgenstern have commented on the segmentation of labor markets in which black men and

---

*Potential labor force is the size of the labor force at full employment.

women fare poorly relative to central-age white males. Because the unemployment rate itself does not provide enough information about the unemployment experience, they have computed duration and turnover of unemployment from the Work Experience Survey that is conducted annually as an adjunct to the March Current Population Survey. For the period 1964-1970, the high unemployment rates of black women were attributable almost entirely to their higher turnover, that is, the frequency with which they become unemployed. Older black women experience unemployment patterns similar to those of young black women, but this is not the case among whites.[15]

Bergmann has suggested a microsimulation model in which the actions and interactions of black workers, white workers, and employers are delineated. The outputs of the model are unemployment rates, distribution of the duration of unemployment, vacancy rates, and distributions of the duration of vacancies. The effect of different separation rates on black unemployment rates depends on how much segmentation exists in the labor market. If blacks are for the most part rigidly confined to a segment, the influence of labor turnover is likely to be relatively unimportant. If blacks and whites are seen as competing for the same slots (differential employability), then differences in turnover rates between the races are likely to be a major cause of differences in unemployment rates.[16]

The Urban Institute's simulation model of the demographic composition of employment, unemployment, and labor force participation is an attempt to predict flows for sixteen demographic groups into and out of employment and unemployment. Job search-turnover theory of the labor market visualizes a complex set of dynamically interacting labor markets that are characterized by great heterogeneity of jobs and workers, massive turnover flows in and out of the labor force and between jobs, and limited information that leads to substantial investment in job search activities. The movement of workers is impeded by barriers that are often related to race, sex, geography, and occupation. Blacks enter un-employment twice as often as whites.[17] Job search theory emphasizes voluntary unemployment. Not enough is known about quits versus involuntary termination of black women.

Unemployment rates for local labor markets measure the difficulty of finding jobs. It was only after the decentralization of major manpower programs under CETA and the allocation of billions of dollars to state and local governments that more reliable estimates of local unemployment were demanded. Earlier studies used unemployment rates for Standard Met-ropolitan Statistical Areas (SMSAs), but because so many black women who live in central city neighborhoods, and frequently within poverty tracts, limit their job search ac-tivities to these circumscribed areas, there is an even more urgent need for more precise local unemployment esti-mates.[18] The labor force participation of black women is highly sensitive to labor market conditions. Sawers notes that there is evidence that black and white women function in labor markets that are to some extent separate.[19]

There are two opposing hypotheses about whether the rate of labor force participation among married women increases or decreases in response to rising unemployment. The addi-tional worker hypothesis declares that when the family head becomes unemployed, other members of the family will enter the labor market in order to maintain the level of family income. The discouraged worker hypothesis, on the other hand, asserts that as the level of unemployment rises, women will become discouraged in the job search and will drop out of the labor force.

Does the discouraged worker effect predominate over the additional worker effect for black women? Bowen and Finegan found in their analysis of 1960 census data that the labor force participation rates of major demographic groups declined as unemployment increased, indicating a much stronger response to the discouraged worker effect.[20] Cain later supported this hypothesis of an inverse relation between participation and unemployment except in the case of black wives and female family heads.[21]

During the 1960s and 1970s black women have experienced higher rates of unemployment than their white counterparts and black males. It is likely that the job needs of this segment of the work force will not be adequately met even with larger or more "targeted" expenditures on employment and training programs.

Employment Discrimination

When the labor market is examined to determine which workers experience the most severe burden in terms of employment discrimination, black women workers are perceived as carrying a dual burden of race and sex discrimination. Their status is most frequently compared with white women workers. If their earnings are different after controlling for a number of personal characteristics, racial discrimination in employment is present. When black women are compared with black males with the same level of education and are found to work disprotionately in lower status jobs and earn less, sex discrimination may be the major type of labor market difficulty. However, among researchers who have focused mainly on certain aspects of employment discrimination, there is no consensus on the issue of whether black women suffer more than any other group in the labor market.

Since 1966, detailed statistics have been collected by the U.S. Equal Employment Opportunity Commission on the employment patterns of private and public employers by race, ethnicity, sex, industry, geographic location, and broad occupational categories. These antidiscrimination data have been analyzed by Ashenfelter, Bergmann, Marshall, and others. In the first analysis of these data in 1968, Ashenfelter noted that although the indices of occupational position for minority females were higher than those of their male counterparts, it was difficult to make adequate comparisons of male and female occuptional distributions. "[The] economic meaning of occupations such as clerical worker and craftsman are very different for the two sexes at the level of occupational aggregation available in the EEO-1 data."[22]

Ashenfelter found that educational attainment explains only about one-third of the difference between female occupational indices of the average black and the average Anglo (white non-Hispanic) female. The index of occupational position of black women was almost 85 percent of the Anglo female index in 1966. Although black women were concentrated in low-paying occupations where there was a large proportion of women workers, Ashenfelter concluded that there was less occupational discrimination against black women than against black men.

When Ashenfelter and Heckman reviewed equal employment opportunity data for the period 1966–1970, they found that the relative occupational position of black females had increased from 84.7 percent of the index for Anglo females in 1966 to 88.9 percent in 1970. This 4.2 percent increase was almost twice as large as the increase in the relative occupational position index for black males for the same time period. Ashenfelter and Heckman argued that if the rate of change of the index was maintained indefinitely, black women would have the same occupational position as Anglo women in approximately 11 years, and black males would achieve the same occupational position as Anglo males in 35 years.[23]

This inference of a superior economic status for black women has been challenged by Barbara Reagan. Reagan noted that the comparison of relative occupational indices for black women and Anglo women infers that the occupational distribution of Anglo women provides the normative goal for racial minority women. "When the change in the occupational position of black females from 1966 to 1970 is compared with the change in the occupational position of Anglo males, the index for black women was 43.5 percent in 1970, an increase of 1.8 percentage points. This is only about three-fourths the upward movement made by black men (an increase of 2.3 percentage points). Thus, the inference that the rate of change for black women from 1966–70 is much better than for black men is not warranted . . . Black women continuing at the 1966-70 rate of change would reach the occupational position of Anglo males only in more than 135 years (as compared with 35 years for black men)."[24]

Marshall and Christian, in their study of black employment in the South, found that in 1966 black and white women were concentrated in essentially the same industries. There was no significant relationship, however, between the indices of occupational position for black and white women. The considerable divergence indicated that these women did not work in the same jobs. Outside the South, the indices of occupational position for black women were larger than for either black or white women in the South.

The Marshall study also found that between 1966 and 1969 black women increased their share of all jobs in the South from 9.37 percent to 13.39 percent compared with an increase of 7.38 percent to 9.09 percent outside the South. In spite of occupational improvement, black women in the South were under-represented relative to whites in all occupations except the operative, laborer, and service categories, which comprised three-fourths of the black women workers in the South.[25]

At the microlevel a considerable number of investigations of labor market activities have been undertaken in support of litigation or proposed litigation of employment discrimination cases. These case studies on black women workers have not been analyzed. Prior to the acceptance of sex discrimination as a major national issue, charges of employment discrimination by black women were handled as racial cases. After 1969, the sex discrimination issues reflected the problems of all women workers. As late as 1976, some of the racial cases that had originated in the late 1960s were finally settled. The racial cases typically have been litigated because black women workers, mainly in Southern facilities, were restricted in terms of hiring, training, and promotion. The textile industry in North and South Carolina, the tobacco processing industry, and the utilities industry in several states, provided examples of overt discrimination. The *Payne* v. *Travenol* and

Tippett v. *Liggett and Myers Tobacco Company* cases are examples.

The Travenol subsidiary of Baxter Laboratories facility in Cleveland, Mississippi, was held to have violated Title VII of the Civil Rights Act of 1964 by requiring applicants for operative jobs on the production line to have a tenth-grade education or equivalent. The educational requirement was not adopted until the employer, a producer of pharmaceutical goods, began desegregating its work force after the passage of Title VII. The requirement disqualified substantially more black applicants than white. Even when the black applicants met the educational requirements, the company hired proportionately fewer blacks. Incumbent employees did not have to satisfy the educational requirement, and in a facility where all of the operatives were white prior to 1964, the beneficiaries of this policy were overwhelmingly white.

A twelfth-grade education required for office and clerical jobs and supervisory and technical jobs similarly operated to disqualify blacks in substantially greater number than whites. There seemed to be no tangible relationship between the duties of these jobs or attributes specified by the employer and the level of education required. The employer, through a variety of techniques, some inadvertent, restricted employment opportunities for black women. Black applicants with clerical qualifications were assigned to work as operatives on the production line. No information was posted about vacancies in the clerical, technician, and supervisory positions. A federal district court ordered that Travenol no longer require a tenth-grade education (or GED equivalency) of applicants for operative positions; a twelfth-grade education (or GED equivalency) of applicants for office and clerical jobs, technician jobs and supervisory positions; and a college degree as qualification for the jobs of systems, traffic, or scheduling analyst.[26]

In the *Tippett* v. *Liggett and Myers Tobacco Company* case it was noted that prior to 1965 the bargaining unit jobs at a Durham plant of Liggett and Myers Tobacco Company were divided among six seniority groups based on race and sex.

The groups and their wage scales in June 1965 were:

Local 176, Tobacco Workers International

White Males	$2.33–$3.36/hr.
White Females	$2.29–$2.68/hr.

Local 194, Tobacco Workers International

Black Males	$2.16–$2.56/hr.
Black Females	$2.02–$2.33/hr.

Local 208, Tobacco Workers International

Black Males	$2.16–$2.61/hr.
Black Females	$2.02–$2.12/hr.

Newly hired workers were placed on a job paying the lowest rate in the appropriate seniority unit. An employee could progress up or down the job ladder in his or her seniority unit only. In 1967 the company and the union, under the auspices of a federal antidiscrimination agency, voluntarily negotiated a new seniority system that attempted to eliminate the present effects of past discrimination practices. Racial and sexual lines of progression were abolished.[27]

Detailed information on where black women are employed in internal labor markets is available in the records of consent decrees, under which employers agree to establish affirmative action programs for improving recruitment and upgrading of minorities and women. The implementation of the 1973 consent decree of the American Telephone and Telegraph (AT&T) Company has improved the employment status of black women in the telephone industry. At the end of 1972 AT&T, the largest private employer in the United States, had 83,799 black employees, 9.5 percent of its work force. Three-fourths of the black employees were women who were overwhelmingly concentrated in the telephone operator and clerical jobs. The upgrade and promotion provisions of the consent decree increased employment opportunities for black women. Between 1972 and 1978 the number of black women workers at AT&T increased from 63,333 to 70,028 or by 10.6 percent. Table 4.3 indicates a noticeable shift of black women workers at AT&T into managerial and craft jobs.[28]

Table 4.3 Black Women Employees at AT&T, 1972 and 1978

	December 1972	September 1978
Black Women Employees	63,333	70,028
Percentage of black workers	75.6	73.5
Percentage of women workers	15.2	17.4
Percentage of all workers	8.0	8.8
Black Women Managers[a]	1,753	5,249
Percentage of black managers	48.6	51.6
Percentage of women managers	5.1	10.1
Percentage of all managers	1.1	2.9
Black Women Craft Workers[b]	598	2,891
Percentage of black craft workers	4.9	18.0
Percentage of women craft workers	9.3	13.2
Percentage of all craft workers	0.3	1.0

Source: Final Report, Consent Decree of AT&T, January 1979.
a. Affirmative Action Plan (AAP) job levels 1–3
b. AAP job levels 10 and 9 (Semi-Skilled Jobs), and 6 and 7 (Skilled Jobs).

Other notable examples of consent decrees have been in the steel, airlines, radio and television, publishing, and banking industries.

Public Sector Jobs

As black women have increased their labor force participation and upgraded their occupational status, they have tended to be employed in the public sector, whereas white women have tended to be employed in the private sector. In the 1970 census data, 22 percent of black women in the civilian labor force were employed in federal, state, or local government, and only 18 percent of white women were similarly employed. (See table R.13.) The noticeable presence of black women in public sector jobs, in recent years, is shown in statistics collected by the U.S. Equal Employment Opportunity Commission (EEOC) and the U.S. Civil Service Commission.

In 1974, according to EEOC's survey data on employment in state and local government (exclusive of educational institutions), 269,086 black women were employed on a full-time basis, and an additional 51,523 were part-time workers. The full-time black women workers accounted for 7 percent of all black female state and local employees, 46 percent of all full-time black workers, and 19 percent of women workers. Black women were heavily concentrated in the paraprofessional and office-clerical occupations, in which the median annual salary was under $7,300 compared with $9,146 for all workers in state and local government. (See table 4.4.)

The Civil Service Commission reported 170,674 black women who were employed full-time by the federal government in 1977. These women represented nearly a quarter of all women federal employees and 44 percent of all black employees.[29] It has been estimated that in 1976 black women who were full-time, full-year employees earned 53 percent more in the federal government than in the private economy. The wage premium in state and local government employment was 31 percent. Adjusting for the skill mix, black women workers still had a 30-percent premium in the federal government and a 5-percent premium in state and local government.[30] For years the federal government was the only place where many professional black women could find jobs that matched their capabilities; the employment policies of the federal government were less overtly discriminatory than private employers. Today many of these black women hold senior positions.

Unions

Although discrimination may lower the earnings of black women, the wage rankings of members within a demographic group depend largely on such variables as human capital and unionization. There are relatively wide differences in the proportion of black and white women workers who are union members. In 1977 about 23 percent of black women wage and salary workers belonged to unions compared with 14

Table 4.4 Black Women Employed in State and Local Government, 1974

Occupation	Number	Median Salary
Officials and administrators	3,686	$13,065
Professionals	30,933	11,239
Technicians	24,905	7,823
Protective services	4,437	9,321
Paraprofessionals	78,510	6,997
Office, Clerical	85,946	7,248
Skilled craft	2,296	6,255
Service/Maintenance	38,373	5,803
Total	269,086	$ 7,380

Source: *Minorities and Women in State and Local Government,* vol. I, EEOC, 1974.

percent of white women workers. Black women were mainly in the apparel, retail trade, and telephone communications industries and in service industries such as hospitals and educational institutions. The average (mean) weekly earnings of employed full time black women workers represented by unions was $201. Black women workers not represented by labor organizations earned $150 and white women union members earned an average of $207 each week. (See table 4.5.)

Because of the overwhelming concentration of black women workers in household service jobs until about a decade ago, their union membership may have been limited. However, the dramatic increase of unions in the health service industry (where many minority women are employed) as well as the expansion of the union effort in public sector employment* are trends that may presage an even larger role for unions in helping to improve the employment status of black women.

*District Council 37 of the American Federation of State, County, and Municipal Employees in New York City reported 100,000 members, in 1972; many were minority females.

Table 4.5 Women Wage and Salary Workers in Labor Unions, May 1977

Occupation	Black		White	
	Number (x 1,000)	Percentage of Workers	Number (x 1,000)	Percentage of Workers
White-collar	488	24.7	2,484	12.7
Clerical	266	22.9	1,164	10.6
Blue-collar	299	34.7	1,302	30.1
Service (includes private household workers)	233	15.7	514	9.0
Total	1,021	23.5	4,307	14.5

Source: U.S. Department of Labor, Bureau of Labor Statistics, *Earnings and Other Characteristics of Organized Workers,* Report 556, May 1977.

Summary

Several labor market policies have been examined as a means of improving the position of black women in the labor market. After more than a decade and a half of operation of various federally-funded employment and training programs, we cannot conclude that they have been effective in enhancing labor market opportunities for black women. Some of the difficulty lies in the manner in which the published CETA statistics classify clients. Black women are included in minority status, AFDC recipients, low-income and female groups. Such a statement as "For the nation as a whole, blacks are better served and women worse served (by CETA programs) than their respective proportions in the total pool of unemployed people"[31] does not shed much light on the economic status of black women. The findings on unemployment for black women are relatively simple; unemployment rates for them are higher than for white males and females and black males. (However, during the 1974–1975 recession, black males experienced higher rates of job loss than others in the labor force.) Employment discrimination against black women is composed of generous doses of sex discrimination (experienced by all women) and lingering amounts of racial discrimination.

5

Earnings

In 1977 only 59 percent of all black families were husband-wife families compared with 87 percent of all white families. Although earnings of black wives and other black women workers comprise a large part of black family income, median family income of all black families was only 70 percent of that for black husband-wife families, reflecting that a large number of female heads of families worked at low wages and/or received public assistance. The comparisons of the earnings of black women with white women rather than white men provide a less than satisfactory standard. However, the long-standing tradition of social science research has been to make racial comparisons for the same sex groups. As researchers are able to refine their models and use more sophisticated methodologies, broader comparisons can be made.

Earnings of Black Women

Despite the improvement in their educational attainment, the upgrading of their occupational status, and the significant shift from part-time to full-time work, the earnings of black women workers are the lowest of all workers in the labor market. Over a 37-year period, 1939–1976, the median wage or salary income of black women who worked year-round, full-time increased from 38 percent of the income for white women year-round, full-time workers to approximately 94 percent. During this same period, the earnings of black men moved from 45 percent to 74 percent of white males. (See table 5.1.) Thus, many researchers have attempted to prove their case of an income advantage for black women by stating that black women have gained on white women faster than black males have gained on white males. They rarely note that the median earnings position of white women vis-a-vis both white and black males has deteriorated; the median earnings of black women have lagged behind those of black

Table 5.1 Median Earnings of Year-Round, Full-Time Wage and Salary Workers by Race, 1939 and 1976

Race/Sex	1939	Percentage of White Male Earnings	1976	Percentage of White Male Earnings
White males	$1,419	100.0	$14,071	100.0
Black males	639	45.0	10,496	74.5
White women	863	60.8	8,285	58.9
Black women	327	23.0	7,825	55.6

Sources: U.S. Department of Commerce, U.S. Bureau of the Census, "Money Income in 1974 of Families and Persons in the United States," *Current Population Reports,* Series P-60, Table 68, 1976; and U.S. Department of Commerce, U.S. Bureau of the Census, "Money Income in 1976 of Families and Persons in the United States," *Current Population Reports,* Series P-60, Table 56, 1978.

Note: Black includes black and other races in both years.

males (about one-half of black male earnings in 1939 and approximately three-fourths in 1976); and in both 1939 and 1976 black women, absolutely and relative to other workers, were at the bottom of the earnings hierarchy. (See figure 5.1.)

The median earnings of women in both full-time and part-time jobs, as shown in table 5.2, include wages and salaries as well as self-employment income. The figures show a fluctuation in the black/white ratio during the 1970s. The apparent reversal of the black/white ratio for 1976 for black and white women with work experience does not represent a significant shift. Census Bureau specialists noted that black women have more work experience than white women, and even though they may work part-time, they may be paid more based on seniority; black women may work longer hours, eight hours instead of four hours; and there might be more white women who are intermittent workers and work in seasonal activities. In March 1977 two important modifications were made in the Current Population Survey, on which these statistics are based: "These changes involve the use of (1) an expanded sample of households, and (2) refined interpolation procedures for calculating median incomes and their respective standard errors."

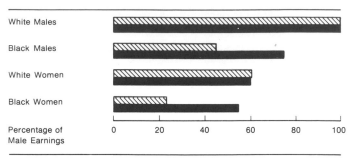

White Males	
Black Males	
White Women	
Black Women	
Percentage of Male Earnings	0 20 40 60 80 100

Figure 5.1 Median earnings of year-round, full-time wage and salary earners by race and sex. Shaded bars represent 1939 data; solid bars represent 1976 data. See table 5.1 for statistics.

Table 5.2 Work Experience and Median Annual Earnings of Women, 1970–1976

| Year | With Work Experience | | Full-Time Workers | | Part-Time Workers | |
	Black	White	Black	White	Black	White
1970	$2,344	$2,800	$3,425	$4,198	$ 682	$ 740
1971	2,376	3,064	3,637	4,446	641	842
1972	3,042	4,190	4,016	4,671	794	873
1973	3,030	3,229	4,107	4,967	802	981
1974	3,368	3,658	4,787	5,363	909	1,124
1975	2,843	3,952	5,331	5,906	1,178	1,286
1976	4,555	4,259	5,916	6,389	1,304	1,362

Source: U.S. Department of Commerce, Bureau of the Census, *Money Income of Families and Persons in the United States.* Current Population Reports, Series P-60, No. 80, 85, 97, 101, 105, 114.

Note: Women are considered to be fourteen years of age and over.

Median earnings may vary in accordance with age, occupation, region of the country, marital status, and educational attainment as well as race and sex. In their study, Levitan et al. paid special attention to the cohort age 25 to 34 because they have benefited the most from recent educational improvements and expanding job opportunities. Because the mean earnings of black women in this age group were 88 percent of the mean earnings of white women of this age group in 1969, the authors adjusted for education within occupations and found that the income of the black women was 110 percent of the white level.[1] They did not, however, specify how they arrived at this figure. Using the same census data that Levitan et al. used, we calculated the mean earnings that black women would receive if they were distributed in job categories in the same way as whites: their earnings were only 97.7 percent of the white mean earnings.[2]

Median earnings for all college-educated black women, however, are higher than for all white women with the same level of educational attainment. There is some indirect evidence in the National Longitudinal Survey data that the interrupted work histories of white women may account for much of the gap in the incomes of black and white professional women. These data also show that older black women professionals have a higher average labor force participation rate than white women, which would account for increases in the hourly rate of pay. Because whites have a lower, average labor force participation rate and earnings are directly correlated with the labor force participation rate, the ratio of black women's earnings to white women's earnings is probably higher than what it would be if only women with similar average labor force participation rates were compared.[3]

The case of black public school teachers demonstrates the need for further research on earnings of well-educated black women workers. According to the 1970 census, primary and secondary teachers accounted for about 46 percent of black women employed in the professional, technical, and kindred occupations, and these black women had median earnings that were slightly higher than those of white women who worked in 1969. Black teachers completed a median of 16.5 years of school compared with 16.6 years of school for all teachers. Almost two-thirds of the 167,174 black teachers resided in the South. Their uninterrupted work histories and investment in human capital contributed greatly to their increased earnings. Sixty-five percent of those in the experienced civilian labor force who had worked in 1969 were over 35 years of age. Thus most of them had worked in the segregated school systems that existed prior to the 1954 school desegregation decision, and in these segregated markets they had been paid less than white teachers in the same system.

It is odd that the earnings gap between these women could have been closed. The story that needs to be documented, and could be by archival materials from a variety of sources, is that large numbers of these black women attended schools in the North (mainly schools of education) during the summer months and slowly acquired enough points to receive graduate degrees. The incentive for this investment was a small incremental increase in annual salaries. Wage data from these segregated school systems, summer school credit hours from such institutions as Teachers College at Columbia, New York University, and some of the predominately black schools (Howard, Hampton, Fisk, Atlanta University), as well as records from the black teachers' associations would reveal more about how these black women teachers were able to transform their education and work experience into relatively high levels of income.[4]

Findings from a recent analysis of the impact of work experience on the labor force activity of mature women (30–44 years of age) based on the National Longitudinal Survey are consistent with the hypothesis of longevity of employment as a major explanation for the racial differential returns to schooling for college-educated black women. A study by Hudis concludes that interaction effects of work experience with schooling and occupational status account for part of the racial differences in wage returns to these two factors. "A considerable part of the observed difference in returns to schooling is due to the higher rate of income return received by well-educated black women with substantial work experience."[5]

The impressive relative earnings gains of black women workers is associated with the *type* of employment discrimination faced by black women. Is it primarily sex discrimination or race discrimination* or do black women workers face a double jeopardy of race *and* sex discrimination? Oaxaca examined the year-to-year variations in black male/black female differentials in median earnings of year-round, full-time workers for the period 1955–1971 and found that the earnings ratio diminished at the rate of about 2.1 percent a year and was statistically significant at the 0.01 level. Oaxaca estimated that all of the gross annual percentage reduction in black male/black female earnings differential could be attributed to the reduction in sex discrimination against black females. The fact that black women gained access to traditionally white female jobs at a faster rate than black males gained access to traditionally white male jobs may have largely accounted for the reduction in the black earnings differential.[6]

The Ruggles study, from a different data base, emphasizes the fact that black women workers are at the bottom of the economic heap. Based on the Longitudinal Employee-Employer Data (LEED) file of the Social Security Administration, which includes information on age, sex, race and earnings for a one percent sample of the social security file, the Ruggles were able to track individuals during the period 1957–1969 and examine sex and race differentials in age-earnings profiles and birth cohort patterns of earnings, work histories, and distribution of earnings.[7]

Black females averaged an increase of 107 percent in their earnings over the period 1957–1969 and, in almost every age

*Nancy Barrett, a discussant on the Oaxaca report, more appropriately terms this "differential rates of change of racial discrimination by sex."

group, exceeded the increase shown for other race or sex groups. However, the level of age-earnings profile for black women was lower than for any other group. The work histories of black women differed from those of white women and males. The employment of black women in the earlier years was substantially lower, but it increased steadily even during childbearing ages. At 25 years of age it equaled that of white women, and it continued to rise thereafter. In 1968, the LEED file showed that 51 percent of black women were in the lowest income class, that is, under $3,000. This compared with 34 percent of black men, 39 percent of white women, and 20 percent of white males.[8] Nancy Barrett, a discussant on the Ruggles study, cautioned that "Although labor force participation rates are higher for low-income women during the childbearing years, labor force *attachment* is stronger for higher-paid women . . . [It] is labor force attachment not the participation rate of a cohort that is most likely to affect its age-earnings profile."[9]

Contribution of Wives to Family Income

Due to the difficulties that black husbands experience in the labor market, such as a greater frequency of unemployment, lower labor force participation, and limited wage and salary increases, the primary emphasis of working black wives has been on maximizing family income. Earnings generated by black wives make up a large part of black family income.

The labor force participation rates of working black wives was 58 percent in 1978, more than double that of 1940. The increased employment activity of black wives is also reflected by the rising proportions of black husband-wife families with both spouses in the labor force. In 1965 about two-fifths of the black families with a working husband also had a working wife. By 1976 two-thirds of these families had a working wife. The earnings of black wives tend to be closer to their husbands' than is the case among white couples. In 1976 black married women who worked year-round, full-time; had median earnings that were 73 percent of the median earnings of black married men who worked year-round, full-time; white married women earned only 54 percent.[10] Behind these relationships is the fact that black men earn considerably less than white men, whereas black women's earnings are much closer to white women's earnings. Nevertheless, in 1976 black wives contributed 34 percent of the family income compared to 26 percent for whites. Seventy-six percent of the black wives contributed 20 percent or more of the family income; fifty-eight percent contributed 30 percent or more, and 38 percent of the wives contributed 40 percent or more of the family income. (See tables R.14 and R.15.) Fewer black married women than white contributed less than one third of the total family income. This means that black married women were more influential than whites in pushing their families to higher income levels.

Another way to determine the importance of the wives' contribution to family income is by examining the median family income by the earning status of husband and wife. In 1976 black husband-wife families in which the husband was the only earner had median family incomes that were 66.6 percent ($9,824) of their white counterparts. However, black husband-wife families in which both were earners had median incomes that were 87.8 percent ($15,744) of their white counterparts. For black families with two earners, in which the husband was under 35 years of age, the ratio of median income was even higher.[11]

Relative Economic Status
of Black Women

Much of the controversy over the relative economic status of black women is not associated with their earnings (wages and salaries) but with their money income derived from other sources. A broad definition of relative economic status includes income from all sources. White women receive more income from social security, private pensions, annuities, and alimony than black women. Black women receive more public assistance and welfare payments.[12] Nevertheless, for both blacks and whites, earnings comprise the bulk of money income.

Although much attention has been given to the ratio of black and white family income, a more interesting comparison is their median income by type of family. Table 5.3 shows that the black/white ratio ranges from a high of 87.8 percent for husband-wife families with both spouses as earners to a low of 61.6 percent for families headed by women. Within the black family structure, the median income of husband-wife families with both working ($15,744) is three times the size of the median income of families headed by women ($5,069), and the latter is one-half of the median income of families headed by men. The median family income of black families has not improved relative to white families due to the increase of female-headed families with low incomes and the decline of two-earner families, particularly for the husband-wife category.

Traditionally, the economist's view of black/white earnings differentials has focused on unequal returns to a given set of market-valued characteristics. A primary distinguishing characteristic between black and white women, however, may instead be access to and the cost of acquiring those market-valued characteristics. According to Loury, if the acquisition of such characteristics depends on the socioeconomic status of the individual's family and community of origin, the relative economic deprivation of blacks in the past will act as an externality inhibiting their future gains.

In the past when white women, by and large, did not work, such background advantages were not important. However, with increasing labor force participation of white women and expanding occupational opportunities (outside clerical work), background advantages are likely to become more important. This may be particularly true given the recent claims of the collapse of labor market discrimination because of convergence of coefficients in black/white earnings equations for younger cohorts. The focus of earnings differentials may shift to identifying more explicitly the set of market-valued

Table 5.3 Median Family Income by Type of Family, 1976

Family type	Income		
	Black	White	Black/White
All families	$ 9,242	$15,620	59.2
Husband and wife families	13,138	16,636	78.9
husband only earner	9,824	14,217	69.1
husband and wife earner	15,744	17,922	87.8
Families headed by women	5,069	8,226	61.1
no earners	3,492	4,077	85.6
head only earner	6,114	7,747	79.0
Families headed by men	10,253	13,619	75.3
head only earner	9,346	13,059	71.6

Source: U.S. Department of Labor, Bureau of Labor Statistics, *Marital and Family Characteristics of the Labor Force*. Special Labor Force Report No. 216, March 1977, Table P.

characteristics and why the level acquired by blacks is lower than that of whites.

Econometric analyses of detailed information on black and white women workers can be used to identify the source of earnings differentials. In the following essay, Linda Datcher applies such a procedure for the period 1960–1970. Datcher shows that most of the earnings gain of black women during this period resulted from a decline in discrimination vis-a-vis white women.

Technical Appendix:
Relative Economic Status of Women,
1960–1970
Linda Datcher

In recent attempts to explain differential earnings of blacks and whites, economists have differed over whether the significant variables are productivity characteristics, such as schooling, or different earnings structures facing blacks and whites, such as employment discrimination. In particular, analysis of earnings data for black and white women provides abundant opportunity for skirmishes on this issue. The results are of major importance in shaping broader social and economic policy.

The one-in-a-thousand Public Use Sample from the 1960 and 1970 census provides detailed information on education, race, marital status, geographic location, hours worked, and family income for all females with earnings. In order to identify the source of earnings differentials between black and white women, separate regressions can be calculated for each racial category. This procedure was used by Joan Haworth in a preliminary study in 1973.[13] Haworth regressed annual earnings on other family income, hours worked, and dummy variables using ordinary least squares. Given that hours is an endogenous variable in an equation for annual earnings, some instrumental variables procedure should have been used to obtain consistent parameter estimates. Some of her findings included:

Black women were much more seriously disadvantaged than white women if they lived in the South.

Black women in 1969 reached their peak earnings at ages 35 to 44, whereas white women's earnings continued to rise to retirement age.

The payoff for education was approximately equal for both races in both years.

Gains made by black women because of changes in human capital came from the entry of young black women into the labor force with productivity characteristics similar to those of young white women and the exiting of older black women who had less human capital than white women of the same age.

In order to determine the relative impact of eliminating differences between races in the levels of earnings-related variables versus eliminating differences in the earnings structures facing the races, Haworth examined two hypothetical black/white earnings ratios. The first assumed that black and white women had equal earnings-related characteristics but retained their respective earnings functions. The second assumed that the differences in their earnings-related characteristics persisted but the earnings function for both races was equal. The hypothetical black earnings for 1969 (based on black means and black earnings function) and hypothetical white earnings for 1969 (based on white means and black earnings function) have been recalculated in tables 5.4 and 5.5 because of errors in the original calculation. (Haworth calculated hypothetical white income in 1969 to be $3,988 instead of $3,853 and black income to be $3,469 instead of $3,415.)

From table 5.5 it is clear that in 1959 the elimination of racial differences in the levels of the earnings-related variables would have generated greater improvement in black relative to white women's earnings than eliminating differences in the earning structures. However, the percentage gain from the former is only slightly higher than the latter in 1969. In addition, table 5.4 shows that the white women's earnings function yields a better payoff than the black women's function. When white women's mean values are substituted into the black earnings function, the resulting earnings are lower than for the white function, $3,853 compared to $4,023 in 1969 and $2,455 compared to $2682 in 1959. Similar results hold for black women.

Another issue that Haworth examines is the relative contribution of improvement in the labor market preparedness of blacks versus the contribution of improvement in job opportunities to black women's earnings gains in the 1960s. The methodology she uses involves comparing the 1959 coefficient of a race dummy variable when earnings of black and white women are regressed on several earnings-related characteristics to the 1969 dummy variable for the same regression. Because the dummy changes only a small amount between 1959 and 1969, she concludes that changes in the black/white earnings ratio between the two years for women with similar characteristics were small, and therefore, that most of the gains made by black women reflect greater labor market preparedness.

Table 5.4 Hypothetical Earnings for Black and White Women

	$\hat{b}\bar{x}$	$b\bar{x}$	$\hat{b}\bar{x}$
Schooling	4100.5	3915.6	3728.0
Age			
14–24 years	−279.9	−170.7	−210.7
25–34 years	−43.0	−69.5	−57.4
45–54 years	17.9	−17.5	16.7
55–64 years	36.3	−41.5	30.8
65+ years	−15.7	4.7	−11.8
Married	−267.6	94.3	−224.6
Once married	−62.5	55.4	−102.3
Rural	−86.7	−24.0	−51.6
South	−114.1	−427.9	−204.9
Other family income	−144.4	−43.7	−93.7
Hours worked	2808.7	1945.0	2887.3
Intercept	−1927.0	−1806.0	−1927.0
Total	4022.5	3414.5	3778.8

$\hat{b}$ = vector of coefficients of 1969 white women's earnings function.
b = vector of coefficients of 1969 black women's earnings function.
$\hat{c}$ = vector of coefficients of 1959 white women's earnings function.
c = vector of coefficients of 1959 black women's earnings function.
$\hat{x}$ = vector of 1969 mean values of white women's earnings-related variables.
$\bar{x}$ = vector of 1969 mean values of black women's earnings-related variables.
$\hat{z}$ = vector of 1959 mean values of white women's earnings-related variables.
$\bar{z}$ = vector of 1959 mean values of black women's earnings-related variables.

$b\bar{x}$	$\hat{c}\hat{z}$	$c\bar{z}$	$\hat{c}\bar{z}$	$c\hat{\bar{z}}$
4306.9	2178.0	1870.4	1848.0	2204.4
−226.7	−138.7	−88.8	−98.7	−124.8
−52.1	−29.4	−37.2	−41.7	−26.3
−18.7	31.0	8.0	28.4	8.7
−49.0	27.1	18.3	22.1	22.4
6.3	−10.5	26.7	−8.4	33.4
112.3	−207.2	−71.7	−183.1	−81.2
33.8	−83.0	−52.0	−148.3	−29.1
−40.3	−71.6	188.1	−57.1	236.0
−238.3	−70.1	−493.0	−148.0	−233.7
−67.4	−78.9	−57.4	−49.2	−92.1
1892.5	1494.8	629.6	1387.1	678.0
−1806.0	−360.0	−141.0	−360.0	−141.0
3853.3	2681.5	1800.0	2191.1	2454.7

Because of differences in the earnings structures between black and white women, adding a race dummy variable is not sufficient to capture the effects of the differences in the earnings variables on black and white women. A dummy variable only reflects changes in the intercept in the regression equations, not in its slope. However, it is reasonable to postulate that if separate regressions were run for black women and white women, there would be substantial differences in the slope of the regression lines; that is, the coefficients as well as the intercepts would be different. Such differences would suggest different structures facing black and white women concerning the effect of the variables on their earnings and/or different tastes between the two groups in their choice of activity given similar circumstances.

In order to construct a more appropriate test of the relative impacts of earnings-related variables and declines in employment discrimination, it is useful to divide changes in the earnings of each group into changes in the levels of the earnings-related variables and changes in the coefficients of these variables. Let

$$\hat{\bar{y}} = (\hat{\bar{x}})\hat{b}, \qquad \bar{y} = (\bar{x})\bar{b}, \qquad \hat{\bar{w}} = (\hat{\bar{z}})\hat{c}, \qquad \bar{w} = (\bar{z})\bar{c},$$

where

$\hat{\bar{y}} =$ mean earnings of white women in 1969,

$\bar{y} =$ mean earnings of black women in 1969,

$\hat{\bar{w}} =$ mean earnings of white women in 1959,

$\bar{w} =$ mean earnings of black women in 1959,

$\hat{\bar{x}} =$ vector of 1969 mean values of earnings-related variables for white women,

$\bar{x} =$ vector of 1969 mean values of earnings-related variables for black women,

$\hat{\bar{z}} =$ vector of 1959 mean value of earnings-related variables for white women,

$\bar{z} =$ vector of 1959 mean value of earnings-related variables for black women,

$\hat{b} =$ vector of 1969 coefficients of the earnings-related variables for white women,

$\bar{b} =$ vector of 1969 coefficients for black women,

$\hat{c} =$ vector of 1959 coefficients for white women,

$\bar{c} =$ vector of 1959 coefficients for black women.

Then

$$\begin{aligned}
\hat{\bar{y}} - \hat{\bar{w}} &= (\hat{\bar{x}})\hat{b} - (\hat{\bar{z}})\hat{c} \\
&= (\hat{\bar{x}})\hat{b} - \hat{\bar{x}}\hat{c} + \hat{\bar{x}}\hat{c} - \hat{\bar{z}}\hat{c} \\
&= \hat{\bar{x}}(\hat{b} - \hat{c}) + \hat{c}(\hat{\bar{x}} - \hat{\bar{z}})
\end{aligned} \tag{5.1}$$

is the difference between mean earnings of white women in 1959 and 1969.

Performing the same operations for black women yields

$$\bar{y} - \bar{w} = \bar{x}(\bar{b} - \bar{c}) + \bar{c}(\bar{x} - \bar{z}), \tag{5.2}$$

which is the difference between mean earnings of black women in 1959 and 1969.

Table 5.5 Estimated Black/White Earnings Ratio for Black and White Women, 1959 and 1969

	1959	1969	Change
Actual earnings ratio	66.8	86.8	29.7
Hypothetical ratio[a]			
no earnings enhancing differences[b]	91.5	95.8	4.3
	82.2	90.4	8.2
no current employment discrimination[c]	81.7	93.9	12.2
	73.3	88.6	15.3
Percent gain from eliminating earnings enhancing differences[b]	37.0	10.4	
	23.1	4.1	
Percent gain from eliminating employment discrimination[c]	22.3	8.2	
	9.7	2.1	

a. The first line in each group uses the white mean values or white earnings function. The second line uses the black mean values or earnings function.
b. Same productivity, but continued employment discrimination.
c. Differences in productivity, but no employment discrimination.

The first term in both equations (5.1) and (5.2) represents the change in the mean earnings that resulted from a change in the coefficients during the 1960s with the earning-related variables constant. A large element in the change in the coefficients may be a reduction in discrimination. Thus the change in earnings from the first part of (5.1) and (5.2) may be taken to represent the change in earnings due to a reduction in discrimination when the earnings-related variables are constant. The second term in each expression would, therefore, represent the change in mean earnings that stems purely from changes in the earnings-related characteristics.

Tables 5.6 and 5.7 decompose changes in the earnings of black and white women between 1959 and 1969 according to equations (5.1) and (5.2). From table 5.6 it is clear that most of the change in earnings for black women during the 1960s was due to a reduction in discrimination, with the major

Table 5.6 Differences between 1959 and 1969 Black Women's Incomes Attributable to Differences in Earnings-Related Variables and Differences in Structures

	b	c	$\bar{x}$	$\bar{z}$	$c(\bar{x} - \bar{z})$	$\bar{x}(b - c)$
Schooling	313.0	167.0	12.51	11.2	218.8	1826.5
Age						
14–24 years	−918.0	−621.0	0.186	0.143	−26.7	−55.2
25–34 years	−291.0	−150.0	0.239	0.248	1.4	−33.7
45–54 years	−89.0	40.0	0.197	0.200	−0.1	−25.4
55–64 years	−355.0	171.0	0.117	0.107	1.7	−61.5
65+ years	175.0	955.0	0.027	0.028	−0.9	−21.1
Married, spouse present	196.0	−150.0	0.481	0.478	−0.5	166.1
Once married	178.0	−147.0	0.311	0.354	6.3	101.1
Rural	−183.0	1140.0	0.131	0.165	−38.8	−173.3
South	−854.0	−913.0	0.501	0.540	35.6	29.6
Other family income	−0.007	−0.014	6247.0	4103.0	−30.0	43.7
Hours worked	1.26	0.44	1544.0	1431.0	49.7	1266.0
Intercept	−1806.0	−141.0				−1665.0
Total					216.5	1397.8

Note: Total difference between computed black women's income in 1969 ($3,414) and 1959 ($1,800) is $1,614.

b = vector of 1969 coefficients of black women's earnings function.
c = vector of 1959 coefficients of black women's earnings function.
$\bar{x}$ = vector of 1969 mean values of black women's earnings-related variables.
$\bar{z}$ = vector of 1959 mean values of black women's earnings-related variables.
$c(\bar{x} - \bar{z})$ = amount of difference between 1969 & 1959 black earnings due to differences in earnings-related variables.
$\bar{x}(b - c)$ = amount of difference due to differences in structures.

Table 5.7 Differences between 1959 and 1969 White Women's Incomes Attributable to Differences in Earnings-Related Variables and Differences in Structures

	$\hat{b}$	$\hat{c}$	$\bar{x}$	$\bar{z}$	$\hat{c}(\bar{x} - \bar{z})$	$\bar{x}(\hat{b} - \hat{c})$
Schooling	298.0	165.0	13.76	13.2	92.4	1830.1
Age						
14–24 years	−1133.0	−690.0	0.247	0.201	−31.7	−109.4
25–34 years	−240.0	−168.0	0.179	0.175	−0.7	−12.9
45–54 years	85.0	142.0	0.210	0.218	−1.1	−12.0
55–64 years	263.0	207.0	0.138	0.131	1.4	7.7
65+ years	−436.0	−301.0	0.036	0.035	−0.3	−4.9
Married, spouse present	−467.0	−383.0	0.573	0.541	−12.3	−48.1
Once married	−329.0	−419.0	0.190	0.198	3.4	17.1
Rural	−394.0	−346.0	0.220	0.207	−3.4	−10.6
South	−409.0	−274.0	0.279	0.256	−4.5	−37.7
Other family income	−0.015	−0.012	9626.0	6578.0	−6.3	−28.9
Hours worked	1.87	0.97	1502.0	1541.0	−36.6	1351.8
Intercept	−1927.0	−360.0			−37.8	−1567.0
Total					34.1	1375.2

Note· Total difference between computed white women's income in 1969 ($4,023) and 1959 ($2,682) is $1,341.

$\hat{b}$ = vector of coefficients of 1969 white women's earnings function.
$\hat{c}$ = vector of coefficients of 1959 white women's earnings function.
$\bar{x}$ = vector of 1969 mean values of white women's earnings-related variables.
$\bar{z}$ = vector of 1959 mean values of white women's earnings-related variables.
$\hat{c}(\bar{x} - \bar{z})$ = amount of the difference in 1969 & 1959 white women's earnings due to differences in earnings-related characteristics.
$\bar{x}(\hat{b} - \hat{c})$ = amount of difference due to changes in the structure.

changes coming in the areas of increased returns to schooling and higher hourly wages. The earnings-related characteristics that were most important to the increase in black women's earnings during the 1960s were increased level of schooling, reduction in the number of black women working in the South, and increased number of hours worked each year. According to table 5.7 the gains in white women's earnings came exclusively from changes in discrimination. As in the case of black women, major jumps in the return to schooling and the hourly wage accounted for most of the increase. Changes in earnings-related characteristics of white women actually lowered their earnings. Therefore, it appears that although the change in the relative earnings position of black women to white women was due to more favorable changes in the earnings-related variables for black women, most of the earnings gains of black women during the 1960s resulted from a decline in discrimination.

6

Special Groups

Three special groups of black women workers experience considerable difficulty in the labor market. Black female teenagers, black women who as single parents have been identified as female heads of family, and black women who work in the household service occupations, are marginal workers in the group of black women workers. These three categories of workers are not mutually exclusive but have been treated as such in this discussion.

Because the labor market behavior of black female teenagers differs so significantly from white young women of the same age and from adult black women, a special comment is needed. Generally the higher work expectations of young black women can be traced to the higher labor force participation rates of adult black women. The greater importance of work as a part of their adult role expectations may stem from differential socialization experiences resulting from higher rates of labor force participation among black mothers, greater instability within black marriages, and anticipated lower earnings among future black husbands.[1]

Nevertheless, young black women, 16 to 19 years of age, have the lowest labor force participation rates, the highest unemployment rates, and the lowest economic status of any group in the labor market. (See table 6.1.) There is some evidence that a disproportionate number of these young black women are single parents with small children. A recent study of unemployment among black teenage females in urban poverty neighborhoods identified their major employment problems as systemic societal impediments, specifically the low priority accorded the black female teenager, and dysfunctional reference groups and motivations. The central

Table 6.1 Labor Force Participation Rates of Young Black Women, March 1977

Marital Status	16–19 years old		20–24 years old	
	Black	White	Black	White
Never married	23.5	51.3	51.9	75.1
Married, husband present	.... a	50.3	65.9	59.7
Other	.... a	51.0	49.7	65.8
Total	24.7	51.2	55.4	66.8

Source: U.S. Department of Labor, Bureau of Labor Statistics, *Marital and Family Characteristics of the Labor Force.* Special Labor Force Report No. 216, March 1977, p. A11.

a. Base less than 75,000.

finding of this study was that peer group support and rein-forcement may be capable of altering some of the outcomes in the labor market for poor, black, young women.[2]

A follow-up study tested, refined, and assessed the labor market–oriented peer group mechanism as an intervention strategy for assisting young black women in their entry into the world of work. This study concluded that the peer group mechanism was especially effective in dealing with the in-tricate and sometimes subtle interplay of race, sex, and age in the labor market orientations and behavior of young black women in a major metropolitan area.[3]

The National Longitudinal Surveys collected data on the labor market activity of young women, 14 to 24 years of age,* both in and out of school.[4] The series of reports on the labor force participation and unemployment supported conclu-sions from Bowen and Finegan that "the staggering amount of unemployment among the youngest black girls, [who were students, was] probably a strong deterrent to labor force entrance among that group," and perhaps the differential in

*After 1967 the official definition of the civilian labor force included only those persons from the noninstitutional population who were 16 years of age and over.

discouragement resulted from racial discrimination by employers. Black women students, regardless of age, as well as black women nonstudents 18 to 24 years of age, were more likely than their white counterparts to be unemployed.[5] There is some evidence that the long-run effects of unemployment among black teenagers is detrimental because it impairs their ability to perform in the labor market later and/or it lessens employers' willingness to hire them for good jobs.

The most recent forecasts of population predict that the black teenage population, unlike its white counterpart, will continue to grow rapidly through 1990. Then the number of young black women 16 to 19 years old in the total population is expected to be almost a fifth higher than in 1970. According to recent forecasts of labor force participation, the size of the gap between black and white female teenagers should decrease not only because of the decline of the white youth population but perhaps because of the greater propensity of young black women to opt for the world of work. Increases in the unemployment rates of young women workers may occur simultaneously with a higher labor force participation if barriers to their full utilization remain in the labor market. More young women in the population may shift from the status of nonparticipant in the labor market to participant, but as an unemployed rather than employed worker. (See the earlier discussion on black unemployment in chapter 4.)

Some might ask why such a small group as the 1.3 million young black women, of which only a third are in the civilian labor force, deserves special treatment in a review of the labor market activities of black women. It is now apparent that young black women do not make the same transition into the world of work as young white women. There is a strong probability that a disproportionate number of black teenagers will become impoverished single parents. Their attachment to the work force may become weaker as the work activity of young white women expands. An understanding of welfare and poverty issues is linked to a continuous study of the labor market behavior of young black women, for teenage mothers are the fastest growing group in the welfare population.

Black Female Heads of Family

According to current Census Bureau definitions, the term female head of family refers to single, widowed, separated, or divorced individuals, not to women who may in fact provide the majority income in a husband-wife household. (A family is defined as two or more persons living together and related by blood, marriage, or adoption.) In 1977, one out of every three black families was headed by a woman compared with one out of nine white families and one out of five Hispanic families.[6] Blacks now account for 28 percent of all female-headed families, up from 21 percent in 1960. Black women heading families were younger, more than twice as likely to be single, and had more children, lower labor force participation rates, higher unemployment rates, higher rates of poverty, and lower educational levels than their white counter-parts. The number of black female heads of families has doubled since 1960, and the most significant change was an increase in the number of never-married heads of families from one in ten to one in five. Thus the special circumstances of these one-parent families require a searching analysis.

Half of the 2.1 million black female heads of families were in the labor force, employed mostly in low-paying, low-skill jobs. (See table 6.2.) Two-fifths of all employed black female heads of families were service workers, whereas 61 percent of white female heads of families were in white collar jobs.[7] The lower median income of black families headed by women, $5,069 compared with $8,226 for white women, reflects not only fewer weeks worked but heavy concentration in low-skill, low-pay jobs. The unemployment rate in 1977 for black female heads (16.4 percent) was higher than the rate for black wives with husband present (9.4 percent) and nearly double the rate for white female heads of families (8.1 percent). Almost half of the black female heads of families

Table 6.2 Labor Force Status of Black Female Family Heads by Marital Status, March 1977

Status	Total	Never Married	Married, Husband Absent	Divorced	Widowed
Population (× 1,000)	2,150	485	705	459	502
Labor force (× 1,000)	1,114	229	390	327	167
Participation rate	51.8	47.2	55.3	71.2	33.3
Employed (× 1,000)	931	163	328	285	154
Unemployed (× 1,000)	183	66	62	42	13
Unemployed rate	16.4	28.8	15.9	12.8	7.8

Source: "Women Who Head Families, 1970–77: Their Numbers Rose, Income Lagged," *Monthly Labor Review,* vol. 101, no. 2, February 1978, Table 5.

had not completed high school. Consequently it is not surprising that 53 percent of black female heads of families, even when their earnings were supplemented by other income, fell below the poverty threshold.

A recent study on female-headed families, *Time of Transition: The Growth of Families Headed by Women* by Heather L. Ross and Isabel V. Sawhill, centers on the role of economic variables in generating or perpetuating female-headed families and their impact on the functioning of these families. The study presents two perspectives for analyzing black families: the situational view and the dysfunctional cultural view of social change. According to the situational view, racial differences in family structure result exclusively from differences in the economic and social circumstances facing blacks. Consequently, if blacks were in the same socioeconomic position as whites, racial differences in family structure would disappear. The cultural view of social change posits that blacks are entangled in a self-perpetuating set of pathological attitudes of an autonomous lower-class culture, and therefore any programs aimed at improving black economic welfare will be severely limited by dysfunctional attitudes.

Neither of these views adequately describes the context in which blacks live. The situational view is too simplistic, not taking into account how the economic and social circumstances that an individual faces will affect both his perceptions of reality and his lifestyle tastes. The dysfunctional cultural view of social change, on the other hand, is a much more static notion of individual behavior. It ignores the fact that, because perceptions, tastes, and behavior described by culture are endogenously formed, changes in the circumstances of individuals will generate change in their behavior.

Ross and Sawhill found that greater marital disruption, lower remarriage rates, and more out-of-wedlock births contributed to the greater prevalence of female-headed families among blacks. In 1970 the greater portion of the racial differences in female-headed families was attributed to higher separation rates. The authors speculate that the continued rapid growth of single-parent families among blacks is related to improvements in health and permissive sexual attitudes raising the fertility of young black women; a combination of the failure of young black men with little education to improve their economic position and the rise in alternative income sources available to the poorest black women; and the increased urbanization of the black population.[8] There is a tremendous need for more and better research on these issues. For most black women, single parenthood is *not* a "time of transition between living in one nuclear family and another."

In 1976 black families headed by women accounted for two-thirds of all black families below the poverty level (1,122,000 black female-headed families versus 1,617,000 black families). Thus, the overwhelming component of black poverty occurs where families are headed by women. Contrary to conventional wisdom, approximately half of all black families headed by women resided in the South. The employment status of black female heads of families has erupted into a divisive issue because these women are classified as the "working poor" if they are employed, although for the most part they may have a weak attachment to the labor market. Because a significant proportion of black female heads of families are also in the transfer system and receive public assistance, a national debate has arisen around their commitment to work efforts.

Many welfare recipients combine work and welfare as sources of income and move back and forth between the labor market and the transfer system. "Women who receive Aid for Families with Dependent Children (AFDC) represent three groups of people: a small group of hard-core unemployed who spend most of all their working years on welfare (10 percent); a larger group who move back and forth between low-income employment and welfare (40 percent); and a final group who are temporarily on welfare because they are down on their luck (50 percent)."[9] Harrison found that 33.8 percent of minority households (adult women and the people who live with them) mixed welfare and work. Thus between 1968 and 1972 one-third of such households received income from both welfare and work, and 84 percent of those that ever had welfare also worked at some time.[10] "When welfare recipients do work, their status in the labor market is low and their gains from employment are minimal."

An issue that has recently emerged in attempts to assess black economic progress is the significance of family background or class status. A better educated, younger, and highly qualified black middle class is developing at the same time a large black underclass survives in worsened economic conditions. Disadvantaged socioeconomic background is now seen by some as a more important determinant of economic attainment than racial discrimination.[11] The increase in the number of black female-headed families with limited economic resources raises numerous questions about intergenerational effects of poverty. It will be several decades before we know the consequences of having 58 percent of 7.6 million black individuals who are below the poverty level (of which 2.8 million are children under 18 years of age) in female-headed families (1976 statistics). Appropriate strategies for assisting members of black single-parent families to improve their life chances have yet to be developed.

The proposed welfare reform package, Program for Better Jobs and Income, announced in August 1977 seemed to treat single-parent families in a "less deserving fashion" than other recipients of income support or benefits.[12] Although single-parent families with children under 7 years of age would not be expected to work, they would neither be trained nor educated. By the time they would be required to work either part-time (children 7 to 13 years of age present in the family) or full-time (no children under 14 years of age), their human capital would have depreciated considerably. Those obligated to work would be guaranteed subsidized public sector jobs at salaries slightly above minimum wages, but the prospects of shifting to the private sector would seem remote.

Under the work and training component of the incremental welfare reforms proposed in 1979, sole parents in single-parent families would be eligible for federally assisted work and training opportunities. It was anticipated that most of the participants in the job and training program under Title II-E of the Comprehensive Employment and Training Act (CETA) would be female heads of families.[13]

Even at high levels of economic activity, those with deficient skills and education and/or other perceived liabilities, experience major difficulties in the labor market. A recent analysis of the economic experience of blacks indicated that black family income gains have eroded in the 1970s due to a dramatic decline in employment of black family heads. "The percentage of black family heads employed the previous year fell from 88 percent in 1967 to 82 percent in 1974. For black female heads the decline was even more dramatic from 62 percent in 1967 to 56 percent in 1974. . . . Since female headed families generally receive less income than families headed by a male, the proportionately greater increase in the number of black families headed by a female has also lowered the ratio of overall black to white median family incomes."[14]

From Domestic Worker to Household Technician: Black Women in a Changing Occupation

Julianne Malveaux

The history of black women as domestic workers is rooted in the slave legacy of black Americans. "House slaves" performed a variety of tasks including personal maid, cook, babysitter, nurse, and companion. After Emancipation, domestic work was one of the few occupations open to black women in the South. In the North, white immigrants dominated domestic work until the stoppage of immigration during World War I. After that, black women worked as domestics in the North as well.

The literature on black domestic workers is sparse, consisting largely of anecdotal accounts, government documents (in particular, a special statistical report issued in 1974 on private household workers by the Employment Standards Administration of the Department of Labor[15]), reports on the Experimental and Demonstration Projects sponsored by the government in conjunction with the National Committee on Household Employment,[16] and magazine and newspaper articles about the inclusion of domestic workers under minimum wage coverage (1974). This skeletal information presents a picture of an occupation in flux.

Trends in Household Employment

In 1970 there were approximately 1.1 million private household workers in the United States. Although blacks were about half of these household workers, there were 600,000 fewer blacks employed in this occupation in 1970 than in 1960. In 1960, over a third of minority women were employed as private household workers, but by 1970 this had dropped to 14 percent. In 1970 the median age of these workers was 50 or more years of age. Their wages averaged only $1.34 per hour in 1971, and short work weeks were more the rule than the exception, with over half working less than fifteen hours in a survey work week in 1971. Most of the black women in private household employment were employed in the South.[17]

The declining participation of black women in the private household occupation was accompanied by rising participation in more remunerative areas in the economy (see table R.6). (The declining participation may also mask statistical error, as some private household workers may not report their occupation or earnings accurately.) In many cases, as the number of private household workers declines, there are demographic indices suggesting that the demand for private household workers should be rising. The rising female labor force participation rate suggests a greater need for household employment.* The rising median age in the country, as well, suggests that if the nation's nursing homes are not to be the sole provider of care for the elderly, a larger number of home health aides will be needed in the future. But the demand for household services cannot be translated into pure demand for household employees. Many services formerly provided by a domestic are now provided by service agencies, such as caterers, laundry services, restaurants, and day care centers.

The Structure of Household Employment

The most striking feature of household employment is its casual nature.[18] Today most household workers still work part-time or seasonally. Hiring is often done through word of mouth, although it may be done through agencies or advertisements. Historically, there were designated streets

---

*Some economists have used the supply of domestic workers as an independent variable to explain the female labor force participation rate. Because so many services are close substitutes for domestic service, it is not clear that this approach is correct. If the duties of the female with children are disaggregated, we might find that women spend the greater portion of their time with child care and that the supply of day care might be a more useful variable than the supply of domestic workers.

where domestics waited while potential employers drove by and chose an employee for the day. State employment services may also act as a clearinghouse for hiring. The casual nature of the household employment and the fact that most household employees work part-time suggests that there are opportunities for combining welfare and other income maintenance programs with household employment. Recent research indicates that work and welfare are intertwined, and some studies have indicated that "rather than two polar types, the 'welfare poor' and the 'working or deserving poor,' we have become aware of a continuum between work and welfare where large numbers of welfare recipients are attached to the labor market either as full- or part-time workers or job seekers."[19]

Furthermore, the casual nature that exists in domestic work suggests that the reported data are not always accurate. Illegal aliens, for example, often hold domestic jobs. Women who are welfare recipients have a disincentive for reporting other incomes (it is deducted from their welfare payments); so they often request that employers not withhold Social Security deductions, even though it is the law for any private household employer who pays more than $50 per quarter.

Because of the irregularity of private household employment and its low pay, private household workers have a high rate of multiple job holding. According to David Chaplin, "The data . . . does not permit one to determine what the distribution of secondary occupation was for those whom private household employment was their primary job, but the aggregated figures suggest that more women came into this occupation as moonlighters than moved in the opposite direction."[20] Chaplin suggests that the decline in private household employment is likely to be overestimated for these reasons.[21] He estimated that there may be an undercount of between 20 and 30 percent in the number of household workers. Not all of these may be welfare recipients. The rising median age of private household workers suggests that many of these women may be Social Security recipients instead.

From Domestic Worker to Household Technician

Low pay is another feature of household employment. Black workers who were full-time, private household workers received less than half the income of other full-time black women. Most of them received no fringe benefits. (See table 6.3.) Some received perquisites such as free meals and transportation on some of the days they worked. Anecdotal accounts of household employment discuss the receipt of used clothing and other household items either in lieu of or as a bonus to salary. Uniforms were provided for a small number of household employees. It is interesting to note that under the Fair Labor Standards Act "the reasonable cost of fair value of some perquisites furnished by an employer may be credited toward meeting the minimum wage requirement of the Act."[22] The fact that most black household workers had annual incomes of less than $3,000 and that most were heads of household may be significant in explaining poverty for some families.

The low pay and casual nature of household employment mean that there is no job security for employees. Household employment, perceived as unskillled, also has little status. Finally, because the structure of the market for household employees is so loose, there is no job mobility or chance for advancement. The household employee who wishes to better herself will usually do so by seeking some other type of employment.

Upgrading Household Employees

The "household services employment problem" was identified as a manpower problem by the President's Commission on the Status of Women in the early sixties. Their concern stemmed from the fact that the occupation, as reviewed, is a secondary one, with low pay, no job security, and irregular work hours and duties. They were also concerned with the declining number of domestic servants. David Chaplin attributes the decline in the number of domestic servants to several factors: "the closing of the supply of foreigners, the equalization of income which has reputedly taken place in the

Table 6.3 Fringe Benefits Received by Domestic Workers, 1971

| | Percent | Distribution of Workers | |
Fringe Benefit	U.S.	South	Non-South
Paid holidays			
None	92	88	95
One or more	7	10	4
Unreported	1	2	1
Paid vacation			
None	90	85	93
One or more days	10	14	7
Unreported	. . .	1	. . .
Paid sick leave			
None	96	94	97
One or more	3	4	2
Unreported	1	2	1
Full or partial payment of health insurance, pension, or worker's compensation	2	3	2

Source: U.S. Department of Labor, Employment Standards Administration, *Private Household Workers,* 1974, p. 33.

United States," and income maintenance programs for the poor or unemployed.[23] Concern about the falling number of household workers and the low incomes of those remaining in the profession, led to an interest in upgrading household employment.

What is striking about the structure of private household work and about the findings of the President's Commission is how little concerns have changed over time. In 1903, Lillian Pettengill published *Toilers of the Home,* a book about domestic workers. She cited social stigma, long and indefinite hours of work, and "lack of incentive because no promotional scale existed" as problems of domestic work.[24] More than sixty years after her book was published, the National Committee on Household Employment (NCHE) was formed "to provide leadership in promoting and establishing standards for private household work; to improve the economic and social status of household workers; to stimulate job development and training programs for household and related service workers; to improve attitudes of employers; and to serve as a liaison with government agencies interested in this field."[25]

The NCHE explored the connotations of job titles and found that a major reason for low status, except pay, may be the title "maid" or "domestic," which implies that the job is a menial one. Recently workers have been referred to as "household employees." Alternate titles suggested by the American Home Economics Association, NCHE, and others include "Foods Technician," "Cleaning Technician," "Home Management Specialist," and "Home Health Aide."

The NCHE, with headquarters in Washington, D.C., organized several local chapters of household workers. A major emphasis was the standardization of the conditions of household employment so that both employers and employees understand the hours of work and tasks required. Also, NCHE has attempted to introduce some of the fringe benefits that are standard in other occupations, such as sick leave and paid vacation. To this end, they have developed a Code of Standards for household employers and employees that covers wages, hours, working relationships, and benefits.[26]

In 1966 the Department of Labor contracted with NCHE to develop pilot programs that would demonstrate methods for recruiting, training, counseling, and placing household workers. Twelve proposals were developed and eight were funded. During the January 1967–March 1971 time period, the following pilot programs operated as part of the National Pilot Program on Household Employment.[27]

Homemaker Service Demonstration, Training Project, Kansas State University, Manhattan, Kansas

Homemaker Training Program, Women's Service Club, Boston, Massachusetts

Household Employment Project, YWCA, Chicago, Illinois

Household Employment Association for Reevaluation and

Training (HEART), Philadelphia, Pennsylvania

Wilmart Services, Inc., Washington, D.C.

Household Workers for Industry, the Ethnic Foundation, Pittsburgh, Pennsylvania

Household Management, Inc., New York, New York

Services United for Responsible and Gainful Employment (SURGE), The Washington Urban League, Alexandria, Virginia

While the eight projects all sought to upgrade and restructure household employment and the image of the domestic worker, each had distinct features so that different aspects of improving the occupation would be demonstrated. The Kansas, Massachusetts, and Illinois projects provided training, placement, and follow-up services for employees, and the Pennsylvania program provided training, placement, and follow-up for both employers and employees. The remaining programs were business oriented, and while they provided training, they were designed to test the feasibility of implementing standards for household service agencies and to determine if such agencies could become financially independent. A goal of the SURGE program in Virginia, in addition, was to become a cooperative household service business.

An overview of the results of the National Pilot Program indicates that it was at least a success for some of the graduates of the training program. Seventy percent of the graduates from all projects were working at the time of the final report, with a high of 97 percent working in Pittsburgh and a low of 33 percent working in New York. Furthermore, the average working graduate received $4,200 per year in pay, plus Social Security coverage, paid vacations, holidays, and sick leave. The average nongraduate, on the other hand, received wages of about $1,400 per year for full-time work. Although most of the Project employers filed Social Security earnings, it is probable that a significant number of household employees were not covered by Social Security.

Data for the results of the National Pilot Program are important in terms of increased earnings potential for trainees, but several stages in the design and implementation of the individual programs are interesting because of their impact on household employment. For example, the four projects that were business oriented did not become self-sustaining during the life of the project. The SURGE project which was designed to test the feasibility of a cooperatively owned venture, was never fully implemented either. These results are not unusual because it takes most new businesses some time to get started. Thus, if the existence of business-oriented projects for household employment are considered important, then a subsidy for part of the costs is necessary.

In the past, businesses that provided maids to private households have been successful but they contributed to present poor working conditions in household employment, particularly low wages and long hours. Maids were recruited from the South by the promise of high wages from employment agencies. After their arrival they were forced to sign contracts making them liable for damages if they worked less than six months. Transportation and other costs were also deducted from their salaries.[28]

While the average household worker in 1970 was above fifty years of age, half of the women recruited by the projects were below forty. Many of them had no previous experience in household employment. This suggests that young women with limited occupational skills and low incomes are interested in household employment if it can be made attractive. Less than a quarter of the women had been welfare recipients, with especially high numbers concentrated in Boston and New York.

Job development was successfully accomplished through the media, which was also utilized for recruitment. Many projects found that there was an overabundance of potential employers willing to pay their wages and adhere to their standards after reading about the upgrading of household employees. As a result of this the projects found that employer training was expensive and unnecessary. Follow-up proved to be a crucial aspect of the projects. Not only were the projects able to clarify work tasks between employer and employee but they were able to increase the feeling of professionalism and decrease the isolation of the trainees by organizing groups of graduates of the training programs. The projects were also able to investigate the broadening of opportunities in household employment. Paraprofessionals trained by the project later became active in the administration of some projects. The Kansas project, which was university-affiliated, defined specialized household occupations and trained women to fill them.

The Trimble report had mixed conclusions about the eight projects. It noted that the National Pilot Project affected employer attitudes about household employment and that it was possible to restructure a previously menial occupation to be more highly paid and more rewarding. On the other hand, the Trimble report concluded that these programs did not have far-reaching effects. While they exhibited the possibility of restructuring household employment, they went no further and there was no follow-up by the Labor Department, which sponsored the projects.*

The American Home Economics Association (AHEA), in a report on career ladders in home economics and related areas, focused on the use of skills acquired in household employment as routes to related careers.[29] For example, a household employee with "preference skills" in foods might, after training, advance to employment in school food services, to catering, or to food preparation and service in restaurants and hospitals. An employee with preference skills in clothing might move to a dry cleaning establishment or to retail trade.

The AHEA report also suggested ways that career ladders (vertical mobility) and lattices (horizontal mobility) might be

---

*The Women's Service Club in Boston, Massachusetts, continues to operate its Homemaker Training Program. It is presently funded through CETA (Comprehensive Employment and Training Act) and trains 60 women per year in 12-week sessions.

institutionalized to expand options for household employees. The suggestions included the development of training manuals and curricula for types of related employment, marketing research to assess supply and demand for workers in certain regions, and the development of methods for demonstrating and evaluating such a program. While the AHEA report raised interesting questions and suggested a variety of paths for "career" household employees, the proposals have only been implemented to a limited extent in the National Pilot Program.

Unionism has been another strategy suggested for upgrading household employment because union organization has often been used to raise wages and status in other occupations. Other workers, such as garbage collectors, receive salaries at or above the median income for salaried employees because of the strength of municipal unions. In addition, the past decade has seen a rise in low-wage unionism. Jack Barbash reports that "the service Employees have increased their reported membership by almost 60 percent, the Laborers by 31.2 percent, Retail Clerks by 76.9 percent, the AFSCME [American Federation of State, County, and Municipal Employees] by 111 percent, Retail, Wholesale, and Department Store Union by 23.3 percent. These compare to the general increase in union membership during this period of 12.5 percent."[30]

Local 1199, the drug and hospital union, is an example of the growth of unionism in the low-wage service industry. Originally the pharmacist's union in New York, it expanded in response to a 1959 proposal to include hospital workers (who are largely minority workers). Other 1199 members include library, dining hall, and computer center workers at educational institutions. An interesting by-product of the organization of low-wage workers has been the opportunity for minorities to become involved in union leadership.

While union organization has improved the status of some low-wage workers, its effectiveness in the domestics area is yet to be tested. Although there may be no legal constraints to prevent domestics from organizing (in 1974, in fact, New

York passed a law specifically allowing maids to form unions and bargain collectively), several institutional constraints suggest that unionizing domestic workers might be only marginally successful.[31]

Unionization of domestic workers would be an expensive and difficult task because of the fragmented labor force for household work, the geographical mobility of workers, and the proportion of casual laborers in the industry. Some of these factors are shared with other unionized industries, such as construction, which overcomes the fragmentation of the labor force by operating a hiring hall. But strikes of construction workers are far more practical than a strike of household workers could be. There would be little pressure involved in a household employee's strike because employers could easily substitute their own work or that of student "strikebreakers" for the work of a domestic. In addition, enough household services are fragmented so that laundry can be sent out, and meals purchased at restaurants. Furthermore, the traditional striker's weapon, the picket, would not be effective because of the number of employees involved.

A thrust in upgrading the status of household workers came in 1973 when Congress amended the Fair Labor Standards Act to raise the minimum wage from $1.60 to $2.00 per hour for most workers. At that time coverage was expanded to include household employees. The coverage of household workers under minimum wage laws does not necessarily improve the wages of domestic workers. The casual nature of employment makes enforcement difficult. Furthermore, the Fair Labor Standards Act does not mandate benefits such as vacation and sick pay, which are customary in most full-time employment but usually nonexistent for domestics.

The thrust toward upgrading household employees, although strong in the sixties, has become somewhat weaker as the problems of high unemployment and inflation have become prevalent in the seventies. Efforts to upgrade household employment through both federal programs and attempts at restructuring the occupation have served more to enlighten the public than to substantially change the status of the household employee. These efforts may have come too late, as black women have had increased access to other occupations. Low-wage unionism in these occupations benefits the woman who has skills similar to the household employee but offers more regular arrangements in terms of hours and duties.

In addition, because many household employees prefer employment that is casual so they can combine their earnings with other sources, the efforts of upgrading will not be felt. The presence of a large number of household employees who do not report their earnings makes it impossible for us to measure this effect.

Finally, efforts to improve the lot of private household workers has several inherent contradictions: "Throughout the years . . . there have been two contrasting and implicitly conflicting themes: (1) improving private household service for the benefit of middle and upper class (and more recently lower class) women, and (2) helping private household workers improve their own situation. The two goals could theoretically be synonymous, but not so easily in practice. To begin with, one of the best ways to help private household workers as individuals would be to help them escape such employment."[32]

Future Trends in Household Employment

In his study, "Labor Supply for Lower Level Occupations," Harold Wool[33] projected that the number of service workers would grow by about 15 percent between 1970 and 1980 and then grow by 2 percent between 1980 and 1985. His figures for service workers are aggregated to include private household workers. In a supplement to the Wool study, J. Peter Mantilla concluded that "Fewer maids will be employed per household and in absolute numbers. Fewer women will choose to work as maids. Wages of maids will continue to rise relative to most other wages and prices in the economy."[34] In making this finding, Mantilla found that the rising educational level of blacks, rising AFDC benefits (particularly in the

1960s), and improved opportunities for alternative jobs (such as janitors) were responsible for the decline in the supply of maids. Mantilla also found that decreasing supply, which leads to rising costs, will cause consumers to substitute their own work, appliances, and commercial services for household employees.

Both the Wool and Mantilla findings indicate a contraction in the legitimate market for household maids in the future, but it is unclear what future projections suggest regarding those household employees who did not show up in the data. Given the rising age of household employees, it is possible that as many of these women collect Social Security, they will enter the "illegitimate" or unreported market for household maids. If this is the case, the legitimate sector could disappear over time, leaving a totally unreported sector of household employees. The question of reporting occupation is an interesting one and should be studied further.

The effects of the rising female labor force participation rates on household employment have yet to be studied fully. Will an increase in female LFP result in an increased demand for household employees (many sources assert this, but there is no evidence, such as higher wages, to bear this out); day care; commercial services, such as laundry, caterers, and restaurants; or in an increased demand for appliances and convenience foods?

For some families in need, emergency homemaker services have been provided by city welfare or family service departments. In many cases, the city contracts with an agency to provide homemaker services. The use and effect of these services on the household employment market should be studied.

The effect of the minimum wage on household employment has not yet been studied, nor have there been follow-up studies on the graduates of the National Pilot Program. In each case, it would be interesting to see what the result of upgrading efforts has been.

In addition, it would be useful to view the institutions (such as AFDC, Social Security, and tax deductions for child care) that influence the unreported status of several domestics. Perhaps the structure of these institutions could be altered to encourage reporting by household employees. Furthermore, the casual nature of domestic work provides an interesting case study in ways to combine sources of income.

Private household employees arc only 1.5 percent of the work force, and this may account for the only passing interest that researchers have had in this area. But domestics are disproportionately female, black, and poor, and their presence in the work force may affect the work status of others. The flow of former domestics to similar but more regular, service jobs lays the groundwork for research in occupational growth. Further research about household employment will give us a more complete picture of women and work.

7

Conclusions

Although the pertinent economic literature on the labor force participation of black women seems to be contradictory, it confirms that there are significant differences in the labor market activity of black and white women. Different analyses of essentially the same data bases have emphasized competing hypotheses. For black women workers, the negative effects of racial discrimination in employment, deficiencies in their human capital, inadequacy of the earnings of black husbands, the structure of black families, and characteristics of urban labor markets tend to offset gains in educational attainment, the significant shift to full-time work, improved employment opportunities as a result of federally funded employment and training programs, and the implementation of affirmative action programs.

Research Suggestions

From this survey of recent economic research on black women workers we have developed a perspective on their labor force participation and work experience activities. Our analysis reveals no typical black woman worker. Instead, there are several stories to be told. A select but small number of college-educated women (11 percent) are mainly professional workers with a high propensity to work. Thirty-eight percent of all black women workers have graduated from high school and an additional 13 percent have completed from one to three years of college; these are younger women, many of whom are clerical, sales workers, or technicians. Another 38 percent of black women workers in the civilian labor force have not completed high school. Many are older women still concentrated at the bottom of the occupational hierarchy.

We have tried to view black women workers as members of families, working mothers, and major contributors to the economic welfare of the black community. The interplay between the black woman's family role and work role has been full of tensions in the past and may or may not be transformed as employment discrimination against black males is diminished. The dramatic changes in the composition of black families during the 1970s, almost two-fifths comprised of female heads with very low income, has had a profound effect on the economic status of blacks. The decline in the proportion of black families with multiple earners, a reversal of an historical pattern, also has exerted a disproportionate impact on black family income.

The interaction effects of race and sex have made it difficult to discern their focal role on black women workers. There is an urgent need to develop a coherent research strategy on the economic status of blacks, especially one that delineates the constructive and central role of black women workers. In the past, the labor force participation rates of black women were high and their earnings contributed significantly to the economic well-being of black families. At the present time, although the more educated and skilled black women hold the same types of jobs as their white counterparts, a large number of poor black women are restricted in their job options or do not participate in the labor market.

Because many of the comparisons made between black and white women are made around either major or intermediate occupational groupings, it would also be useful to focus on the comparative status of women in the detailed occupations. It is possible that the appearance of occupational convergence masks variance within the intermediate occupational groupings. Thus, if black women are concentrated in the lower-skilled detailed occupations of a particular group, the conclusion that there has been movement toward occupational parity is unwarranted. For example, the intermediate census category, "stenographers, typists and secretaries," includes specialized legal and medical secretaries and lower-skilled stenographers and typists. The Survey of Income and Education (SIE) sampled 9,624 persons in this category and 4.9 percent of them (472 persons) were black. Only thirteen, or 2.3 percent of the legal and medical secretaries sampled were black, but 9.2 percent of the 1,396 stenographers and typists were black.

A comprehensive research strategy could possibly determine the causes of the substantial deterioration of the relative economic status of black women and recommend alternative policies and programs. Some specific research suggestions follow.

Work Role and Family Role

Well-educated black women have learned how to balance the demands of the work environment, where they experienced racial and sex discrimination, and the demands of their home. Frequently these women were married to men who held lower-status jobs. With the increased labor force participation of married white women, is there anything that they might learn from the experience of well-educated black women who have combined several roles? We think so, and suggest that a large sample of these black women be interviewed in depth. Sociologists or social psychologists would appear to be better qualified than economists to undertake such a project. We recommend that the project be conducted under the aegis of several national black sororities. The case study of the black teachers mentioned in chapter 5 could be developed. A possible explanation for the high black/white income ratio among professional women and their longer, more consistent labor force participation could be documented. These data could provide some insight because members of these organizations are the successful black professional women.

Working Poor

"The low-wage employed have several shared characteristics that differentiate them from the general work force. They are generally young, primarily women, and/or members of a minority race. More often than not, they are low-skilled, have little education, and frequently work only part-time."[1] Several studies have used the University of Michigan's Panel Study of Income Dynamics in order to examine the processes of change in the economic status of low-income individuals.[2]

Because more than a quarter of all black women (25 to 64 years of age) in the experienced civilian labor force in 1970 were classified as nonhousehold service workers (cleaning, food, health, and personal services), we need to know more about these women whose median (and mean) earnings, even when they worked 50 to 52 weeks, were approximately $3,500 in 1969. (The poverty level in 1969 for a nonfarm family of four persons was $3,743.) They were largely in the 35–44 age group with limited education; however, the government manpower programs generally emphasize providing work experience or acquisition of skills for younger women. These older women will probably work in these low-wage industries for the remainder of their time in the labor force. We need to know more about the impact of minimum wage, unemployment insurance coverage, unionization, and other labor market programs on the employment status of these older women.

Teenagers

Black female teenagers (16–19 years old) experience the highest unemployment rates and the lowest labor force participation rates of any group of workers. Yet the programs included under the Youth Employment and Demonstration Projects Act of 1977 (YEDPA), with few exceptions, have not given adequate attention to the needs of these young women. The Youth Incentive Entitlement Pilot Program is one of the major demonstration programs established under YEDPA to provide work experience and/or employability development services for economically disadvantaged youth. This program guaranteed part-time jobs during the school year and full-time jobs during the summer to 16–19 year olds from low-income families. The entitlement was designed to encourage such youth to remain in school, return to school, or enroll in equivalency education programs. Findings on the impact of the Entitlement Program on labor force participation, employment earnings, and education will not be available before 1982.[3]

Work and Welfare

Although the emphasis in this report has been on black women who work, we are aware of the problems of nonparticipants in the labor market. What do we know about decisions to leave or enter either the labor market or the transfer system? Is there some quasi-market activity by these women, that is, nonreported Social Security earnings? The findings from studies of the behavior of participants in experimental programs that guarantee minimum income may provide important insights into the work/welfare nexus. The preliminary results from the Seattle and Denver Income Maintenance Experiments are that recipients of the guaranteed stipends worked less than they might have otherwise and their rates of marital dissolution were higher.[4] Obviously, the jury is still out, and many critical reviews will be made of these results before new policies on income maintenance or welfare reform can be formulated.

Black Women Workers in CETA

The sizeable expenditure by the federal government on job creation and training programs under the Comprehensive Employment and Training Act (CETA) for the structurally unemployed, underemployed, and disadvantaged provides an opportunity to examine carefully how black women workers fare in different geographic locations and in different programs and compare state and local operated programs with the national categorical efforts. These data for the past should be analyzed. The Continuous Longitudinal Manpower Survey (CLMS) now being collected for CETA may yield much of the needed information.

Some Policy Suggestions

At a time when women as a group have greatly expanded

their labor force participation rates, the overriding policy concern of this report is how best to increase the work commitment of an important segment of black women: the low-income, female heads of families who differ significantly from other black women workers as well as white women workers. Because 44 percent of the 7.9 million own children under 18 years of age were members of these black families with female heads in March 1977, the issue is confounded. If, for whatever reason the number of black families headed by one parent increases, the primary social policy issue becomes how to increase the capabilities of these women to enable them to provide adequate support for themselves and their children.

These are women whose lack of education, skills, and work experience restrict their earnings in the labor market. Many have made the economic calculus that the transfer system (including AFDC grants, food stamps, Medicaid, and subsidized housing) provides a higher level of economic support for their families than their own work efforts. In order to change this system, market work must be made far more attractive for women. Several short-run suggestions could be adopted without a major expenditure of funds.

Because more income is needed by these women who head families, more of them should be placed in training programs for nontraditional jobs, such as in construction trades and other skilled jobs. The hourly pay rates are up to triple those in the typical female occupations.

Another type of labor market intermediary is needed to help channel workers from Public Service Employment programs into jobs in the private sector. The bridge cannot be made at this time by intermediaries who are perceived as alien to the business environment. These intermediaries would assist both employees and employers through difficult transitions to higher participation in private employment.

Black women workers as well as all other women will benefit greatly from full implementation of laws against sex discrimination. Once there is equal pay for equal work, no differentiation between males and females on fringe benefits, a limitation on separate lines of progression and seniority systems, appropriate maternity and pregnancy leave policies, earnings of women will be increased.[5]

In 1976 approximately 48 percent of the 2.1 million black women who headed families lived in the South and almost three-fifths of these women had family incomes below the official poverty level. (For a nonfarm family of four persons the poverty threshold in 1976 was $5,815.) As this region of the country alters and expands its industrial base, it is important that both racial and sex barriers in employment be eliminated. Also there may be regional solutions found on how to improve opportunities in the labor market for these black women.

Approximately 10 percent of the recipients of AFDC are enrolled in the Work Incentive Program (WIN), but for a number of reasons the WIN program has not significantly increased a greater work attachment among AFDC recipients. A recent demonstration project, the WIN Laboratory Project, may produce some useful techniques. In several selected sites, experimental programs are underway on how best to assist these women in becoming more firmly attached to the labor market.

Some of the problems raised have become intergenerational; thus we wonder how early and what kind of intervention should take place. Better counseling and work-study programs may help to retain young women in the 16–19 year age group in school. Training programs for young mothers out of work and out of school may make it easier to place them in either the public or private sector. Expanded placement of older nonworking female heads of families in jobs may reduce the transfer burden.

Black women workers represent a culture in which a working mother is a normative orientation. There is little reason to believe that black female heads of families "deserve" to be consigned to the bottom of the economic ladder.

We have reviewed the recent employment status of black women, but feel less sanguine about the future. Will better educated younger women now entering the labor market be treated as identical to their white counterparts? This question will remain unanswered for at least a decade as entry level near-parity yields to intense competition for the very few upper echelon positions. If not, will black women occupy the traditional female jobs now predominately held by white women? If white women are not able to shift to the nontraditional jobs, will there be intense competition and overcrowding by black and white women in a few occupations? If the performance of the economy is weak for an extended period, will the black women with limited education and skills bear a disproportionate share of unemployment? What can be done to improve the economic status of the increasing number of female heads of families? Black women have had a long history of discrimination in the labor market. It seems unlikely that within the next decade more than a "token" few will make significant inroads into new occupations and better jobs.

Appendix A

Table R.1 Black Women (16 yrs. and over) in Labor Force in Selected States, 1976

State/Region	Labor Force (× 1,000)	Percentage of Total
Total United States	4,788	100.0
New England	91	1.9
Middle Atlantic	844	17.6
New York	479	
New Jersey	173	
Pennsylvania	192	
East North Central	780	16.3
Ohio	207	
Illinois	284	
Michigan	195	
West North Central	152	3.2
Missouri	104	
South Atlantic	1,457	30.4
Maryland	196	
District of Columbia	114	
Virginia	153	
North Carolina	269	
South Carolina	158	
Georgia	276	
Florida	270	
East South Central	498	10.4
Tennessee	152	
Alabama	160	
Mississippi	131	
West South Central	578	12.1
Louisiana	185	
Texas	293	
Mountain	42	0.9
Pacific	346	7.2
California	326	

Source: U.S. Department of Labor, Bureau of Labor Statistics. *Marital and Family Status of Workers by State and Area,* Report No. 545, Dec. 1978. p. 8.
Note: States with less than 75,000 black women in the labor force are not shown individually but are included in regional totals.

Table R.2 Employment Status of Women by Marital Status, March 1977 (× 1,000)

Race and Marital Status	Total in Population	Total in Labor Force
Black	8,896	4,386
Single	2,530	1,089
Married		
husband present	3,383	1,917
husband absent	1,078	573
Widowed	1,171	311
Divorced	734	496
White	71,799	34,294
Single	13,228	8,188
Married		
husband present	43,775	20,045
husband absent	1,981	1,115
Widowed	8,739	1,911
Divorced	4,076	2,035

Source: U.S. Department of Labor, Bureau of Labor Statistics. *Marital and Family Characteristics of the Labor Force, March 1977.* Special Labor Force Report No. 216, Table A.

| Percentage of Population in Labor Force | Employed | Unemployed | | Not in Labor Force |
		Number	Percentage of Labor Force	
49.3	3,765	621	14.2	4,510
43.0	816	273	25.1	1,441
56.7	1,738	180	9.4	1,466
53.1	488	85	14.8	505
26.6	285	26	8.3	860
67.5	438	58	11.7	238
47.8	31,628	2,666	7.8	37,505
61.9	7,352	836	10.2	5,040
45.8	18,721	1,324	6.6	23,730
56.3	967	148	13.3	866
21.9	1,795	116	6.1	6,828
74.4	2,793	242	8.0	1,042

Table R.3 Women in the Labor Force by Marital Status, Age, and Race, March 1977 (× 1,000)

Race and Age	Total	Single	Married[a]	Other[b]
Black				
Total, 16 years and over	4,386	1,089	1,917	1,380
16–19 years	282	250	23	8
20–24 years	700	397	223	80
25–34 years	1,295	273	649	373
35–44 years	885	89	458	338
45–54 years	734	54	358	323
55–64 years	378	21	180	178
65 years and over	111	5	28	79
Median age (years)	34.3	23.7	36.4	41.7
White				
Total, 16 years and over	34,294	8,188	20,045	6,061
16–19 years	3,594	3,106	408	80
20–24 years	5,575	2,688	2,486	400
25–34 years	8,226	1,318	5,527	1,381
35–44 years	6,070	333	4,633	1,104
45–54 years	5,906	321	4,329	1,255
55–64 years	3,945	295	2,356	1,295
65 years and over	978	127	306	545
Median age (years)	34.7	21.8	38.5	45.5

Source: U.S. Department of Labor, Bureau of Labor Statistics, *Marital and Family Characteristics of the Labor Force, March 1977.* Special Labor Force Report No. 216, Table B-1.

a. Includes married women, spouse present.
b. Includes widowed, divorced, and married, spouse absent.

Table R.4 Civilian Labor Force Participation Rates for Women by Color and Age, Selected Years

Age and Race	1960	1970	1978
Total			
16 years and over			
Black	48.2	49.5	53.3
White	36.5	42.6	49.5
16–17 years			
Black	22.1	24.3	27.7
White	30.0	36.6	48.9
18–19 years			
Black	44.3	44.7	48.6
White	51.9	55.0	64.6
20–24 years			
Black	48.8	57.7	62.8
White	45.7	57.7	69.3
25–34 years			
Black	49.7	57.6	68.7
White	34.1	43.2	61.0
35–44 years			
Black	59.8	59.9	67.1
White	41.5	49.9	60.7
45–54 years			
Black	60.5	60.2	59.8
White	48.6	53.7	56.7
55–64 years			
Black	47.3	47.1	43.6
White	36.2	42.6	41.2
65 years and over			
Black	12.8	12.2	10.7
White	10.6	9.5	8.1

Source: U.S. Department of Labor, Employment and Training Administration, *Employment and Training Report of the President, 1979*, pp. 241–242.

Table R.5 Major Occupations of Employed Women by Color, 1960 and 1970

Occupation	Black Women		White Women	
	1960	1970	1960	1970
Total employed	2,623,724	3,699,448	18,548,577	25,470,679
Professional, technical, and kindred workers	7.5%	11.0%	13.4%	15.3%
Managers and administrators, except farm	1.3	1.5	4.3	3.8
Sales workers	1.7	2.4	8.7	7.5
Clerical and kindred workers	8.4	19.4	32.3	34.8
Craftsmen, foremen, and kindred workers	0.8	1.3	1.4	1.8
Operatives, except transport	12.0	14.2	15.2	12.5
Transport equipment operatives	0.1	0.3	0.2	0.4
Laborers, except farm	1.4	1.3	0.7	0.9
Farmers and farm managers	0.7	0.1	0.5	0.2
Farm laborers and farm foremen	2.9	0.9	0.9	0.4
Service workers, except private household	20.9	21.9	13.0	14.2
Private household workers	34.2	14.1	4.1	2.1
Occupation not reported	8.1	11.5	5.3	6.1

Source: U.S. Bureau of the Census, Census of Population: 1970. *Characteristics of the Population,* vol. 1, part 1, U.S. Summary, Table 81, p. 1-375.

Table R.6 Black Women Professional and Technical Workers (16 yrs. and over) in the Experienced Civilian Labor Force, 1970

Occupation	Number	Percentage of Total	Median School Years Completed
TOTAL	388,960	100.0	16.0
Accountants	7,526	1.9	13.0
Computer specialists	2,794	0.7	15.1
Librarians, archivists, curators	6,738	1.7	16.4
Life and physical scientists	1,443	0.4	16.2
Personnel and labor relations workers	7,023	1.8	13.8
Physicians, dentists, and related practitioners	1,765	0.5	16.3
Registered nurses, dietitians and other therapists	72,960	18.8	12.7
Dietitians	6,961		12.2
Registered nurses	62,799		12.7
Therapists	3,200		13.0
Health technologists and technicians	15,459	4.0	12.7
Religious workers	1,353	0.3	12.6
Social scientists	1,328	0.3	16.2
Social and recreation workers	26,905	6.9	14.7
Teachers, college and universities	7,731	2.0	16.9
Teachers, except college and universities	177,240	45.6	16.5
Elementary school	117,262		16.6
Secondary	38,853		16.7
Prekindergarten and kindergarten	14,852		13.3
Adult education	2,342		15.5
Teachers, except college, not elsewhere classified	3,931		14.0
Engineering and science technicians	5,026	1.3	12.8
Technicians, except health, engineering and science	1,326	0.3	12.7
Vocational and educational counselors	5,623	1.4	17+
Writers, artists, entertainers	7,231	1.9	12.9
All others	39,489	10.2	

Source: U.S. Bureau of the Census, Census of Population: 1970. Subject Reports. Final Report PC(2)-7A, *Occupational Characteristics*, Table 2.

Table R.7 Occupations of Employed Women, 1970

Detailed Occupation	Black Women		Percentage of All Women	White Women	
	Number	Percent Distribution		Number	Percent Distribution
Total employed	3,333,659	100.0	11.5	5,375,301	100.0
Professional, technical, and kindred workers	378,588	11.4	8.3	4,132,696	16.3
Computer specialists	2,720	0.1	5.4	46,476	0.2
Engineers	719	0[a]	3.6	19,037	0.1
Lawyers and judges	394	—	3.0	12,588	0[a]
Librarians, archivists, and curators	6,646	0.2	6.6	92,835	0.4
Life and physical scientists	1,381	—	5.1	24,220	0.1
Personnel and labor relations workers	6,862	0.2	7.5	83,479	0.3
Physicians, dentists, and related practitioners	1,711	0.1	3.9	39,143	0.2
Registered nurses, dietitians, and therapists	71,487	2.1	8.0	811,626	3.2
Health technologists and technicians	15,145	0.5	8.3	162,917	0.6
Religious workers	1,288	0[a]	5.0	24,176	0.1
Social and recreation workers	25,861	0.8	16.4	129,490	0.5
Teachers, college and university	7,535	0.2	5.4	129,242	0.5
Teachers, except college and university	173,502	5.2	9.0	1,746,208	6.9
Engineering and science technicians	4,700	0.1	5.3	82,089	0.3
Writers, artists, and entertainers	6,593	0.2	2.9	219,388	0.9
Managers and administrators, except farm	46,625	1.4	4.4	1,002,272	3.9
Bank officers and financial managers	1,426	0[a]	2.6	52,427	0.2
Buyers, wholesale and retail trade	1,291	0[a]	2.5	50,699	0.2
Health administrators	2,030	0.1	5.4	35,290	0.1
Restaurant, cafeteria, and bar managers	7,564	0.2	6.9	99,862	0.4
Sales managers and department heads	1,701	0.1	2.8	57,662	0.2
School administrators	5,161	0.2	9.4	49,307	0.2
Sales workers	85,081	2.6	4.0	2,038,977	8.0
Sales clerks, retail trade	55,969	1.7	3.8	1,395,734	5.5

Clerical and kindred workers	691,097	20.7	6.8	9,346,947	36.8
Bank tellers and cashiers	51,322	1.5	5.7	846,266	3.3
Bookkeepers	33,445	1.0	2.6	1,228,237	4.8
Secretaries, stenographers, and typists	180,887	5.4	4.9	3,467,719	13.7
Statistical clerks	12,933	0.4	8.2	143,341	0.6
Craft and kindred workers	48,140	1.4	9.3	463,670	1.8
Operatives, except transport	534,154	16.0	13.2	3,442,495	13.6
Clothing, ironers, and pressers	56,042	1.7	41.0	78,089	0.3
Dressmakers, except factory	8,300	0.2	9.0	81,189	0.3
Metalworking operatives, except precision machines	16,450	0.5	10.8	134,392	0.5
Sewers and stitchers	77,604	2.3	9.5	718,636	2.8
Textile operatives	29,154	0.9	12.5	202,744	0.8
Transport equipment operatives	12,937	0.4	9.7	120,008	0.5
Laborers, except farm	48,372	1.5	17.3	228,513	0.9
Farm workers	42,272	1.3	18.1	184,828	0.7
Service workers, except private household	850,455	25.5	17.7	3,892,672	15.3
Cleaning service workers	206,157	6.2	34.6	380,485	1.5
Food service workers	229,123	6.9	12.0	1,656,314	6.5
Cooks, except private household	110,477	3.3	21.2	404,288	1.6
Waiters, food counter and fountain workers	57,202	1.7	6.2	955,360	3.8
Health service workers	225,918	6.8	21.6	808,319	3.2
Health aides (incl. nursing), orderlies, and attendants	172,346	5.2	24.2	531,975	2.1
Practical nurses	49,063	1.5	21.6	175,261	0.7
Personal service workers	82,559	2.5	10.6	685,007	2.7
Child care workers, except private household	17,687	0.5	14.9	100,100	0.4
Hairdressers and cosmetologists	33,424	1.0	7.7	395,645	1.6
Housekeepers, except private household	9,578	0.3	12.8	64,076	0.3
Protective service workers	7,869	0.2	13.3	51,075	0.2
Private household workers	595,938	17.9	52.6	522,223	2.1

Source: U.S. Department of Commerce, Social and Economic Statistics Administration, Bureau of the Census.

a. Rounded to zero.

Table R.8 Occupational Participation Rates of Black Women as a Percentage of Total Employed Women, 1962–1974

Occupational Group	1962	1963	1964	1965
Total employed	12.6	12.5	12.7	12.7
Professional	6.7	7.7	7.9	6.2
Accountants	2.1	3.8	5.7	1.8
Registered nurses	5.2	5.3	4.9	5.1
Social workers	14.1	10.0	7.8	16.1
Elementary schoolteachers	9.8	11.0	10.6	10.9
Managers	3.9	4.1	4.5	4.6
Salesworkers	2.9	3.2	3.4	3.4
Clerical workers	4.1	4.2	4.6	4.7
Bookkeepers	1.5	2.1	2.2	1.9
Cashiers	3.3	3.8	5.4	6.1
Office machine operators	6.5	8.3	9.0	8.9
Postal clerks	13.9	13.6	17.0	26.7
Receptionists	3.8	3.1	2.9	2.4
Secretaries	2.3	2.1	2.6	2.5
Telephone operators	4.1	3.9	4.1	6.3
Typists	8.1	6.8	7.3	7.1
Craft workers	7.8	6.8	8.5	8.0
Operatives	12.0	11.4	11.6	12.2
Checkers and inspectors	3.8	5.2	4.6	6.7
Dressmakers	9.0	8.3	9.4	10.3
Packers and wrappers, except meat	11.5	10.6	9.5	12.2
Laborers, except farm	26.6	20.7	19.8	21.3
Farm laborers and supervisors	27.0	26.7	25.4	24.7
Farm laborers (wage workers)	53.4	53.9	55.1	55.5
Service workers, except private household	18.4	18.3	19.1	20.1
Chamber cleaners	57.5	55.0	56.9	60.8
Cooks	22.9	22.9	22.7	26.7
Food counter workers	11.8	11.3	13.4	12.6
Waiters	6.4	5.3	6.4	6.7
Nursing aides	25.9	26.3	26.1	27.6
Practical nurses	20.0	21.7	25.4	27.3
Hairdressers	14.4	13.7	11.8	11.2
Babysitters	8.3	7.3	7.1	8.5
Housekeeper, private households	27.4	27.7	29.0	28.0

Note: Data for 1962 through 1966 are not strictly comparable with data for later years because 14- and 15-year-olds were included in those years and excluded in 1967 and later years. In addition, data for 1962–71 are not comparable with figures for 1972 and later years because of definitional changes.

1966	1967	1968	1969	1970	1971	1972	1973	1974
12.5	12.5	12.5	12.4	12.3	12.3	12.1	12.3	12.4
8.2	8.2	8.5	9.0	9.1	8.9	9.4	10.2	9.7
4.1	5.0	4.6	5.1	6.6	4.5	6.5	9.9	9.5
6.4	6.9	6.7	6.5	6.3	7.3	8.2	9.7	9.8
17.2	12.0	17.9	15.3	15.9	19.2	19.5	21.1	21.7
11.0	10.6	10.8	11.6	10.8	10.0	10.2	10.1	10.5
4.2	4.1	4.4	4.4	5.3	5.8	6.1	6.6	6.0
3.4	3.6	4.0	4.1	4.4	4.6	4.8	4.5	4.9
5.3	6.2	6.7	7.2	7.4	8.0	8.2	8.8	8.8
2.0	2.5	2.7	2.5	2.7	3.1	3.3	3.9	4.2
6.7	6.7	5.4	6.3	6.7	7.7	7.8	7.9	7.8
6.9	9.2	11.3	11.1	13.2	14.6	13.9	15.7	15.0
32.1	31.5	31.3	29.8	34.5	36.0	28.0	23.5	28.0
4.1	5.2	6.2	5.6	5.4	5.2	7.3	8.4	7.8
2.9	3.6	3.6	3.6	3.7	4.4	5.2	5.7	5.1
5.2	8.4	8.5	9.9	10.5	12.3	12.9	12.1	12.6
8.5	9.7	10.9	13.4	12.0	14.1	12.1	13.6	13.6
8.0	7.4	8.5	9.4	8.7	9.3	9.1	9.3	11.2
13.0	14.2	14.5	15.1	14.9	15.4	14.0	15.0	16.5
5.7	7.5	9.6	9.7	9.7	9.1	9.9	10.3	12.5
8.8	11.8	9.8	12.0	12.0	10.1	8.6	12.2	13.8
12.9	10.5	11.8	13.3	14.4	14.5	15.2	13.1	14.9
19.4	23.1	17.5	20.5	19.9	14.9	12.7	15.4	14.1
29.3	18.2	15.6	13.5	12.6	11.7	9.3	11.4	11.2
44.8	43.5	42.0	37.8	36.4	35.8	25.7	28.5	23.6
20.4	19.5	19.8	19.1	19.0	19.0	18.5	17.8	18.1
60.4	59.4	59.4	56.3	54.7	44.6	42.9	38.3	35.1
28.9	26.5	24.9	24.0	22.7	23.5	21.0	21.3	20.8
13.0	15.2	17.6	10.8	13.8	9.4	9.5	8.7	8.4
6.7	6.2	6.4	5.8	5.0	5.4	5.7	5.5	6.7
27.2	25.0	26.7	27.0	27.5	26.7	27.3	25.4	26.3
25.4	20.4	22.3	23.7	25.5	24.8	25.4	24.6	24.3
9.6	8.2	8.1	8.5	8.6	7.8	7.3	8.5	8.9
7.1	9.1	8.7	8.4	8.3	8.8	9.8	9.6	14.9
29.6	31.6	25.2	27.3	27.9	27.4	27.3	32.4	37.8

Table R.9 Occupation of Employed Black Women (16 years and over) by Region, 1970

Detailed Occupation	Total in U.S.	Percent-age of Total	South
Total	3,309,080		1,707,016
Professional, technical, and kindred	373,713	11.3	188,855
Nurses	59,007	1.8	21,550
Health workers, except nurses	28,619	0.9	10,563
Teachers, elementary and secondary	167,174	5.0	108,372
Technicians, except health	5,895	0.2	2,549
Other professional workers	113,018	3.4	45,821
Managers and administrators, except farm	48,098	1.4	21,947
Sales workers	84,103	2.5	34,169
Retail trade	70,090	2.1	28,451
Other than retail trade	14,013	0.4	5,718
Clerical and kindred	684,310	20.7	218,502
Bookkeepers	31,542	1.0	8,197
Secretaries, stenographers, and typists	178,800	5.4	60,113
Other clerical workers	473,968	14.3	150,192
Craftsmen, foremen and kindred	47,372	1.4	22,748
Operatives, except transport	533,160	16.1	270,784
Transport equipment operatives	13,195	0.4	8,674
Laborers, except farm	49,389	1.5	28,338
Farmers and farm managers	5,646	0.2	3,115
Farm laborers and farm foremen	34,850	1.1	30,613
Service workers, except private household	843,018	25.5	454,529
Cleaning service workers	205,045	6.2	125,850
Food service workers	230,411	7.0	154,648
Health service workers	223,556	6.8	90,307
Personal service workers	79,675	2.4	38,001
Protective service workers	7,860	0.2	2,775
Other service workers	96,471	2.9	42,948
Private household workers	592,226	17.9	424,742

Source: U.S. Bureau of the Census, Census of Population: 1970, vol. 1, *Characteristics of the Population,* Part 1, U.S. Summary—Section 1, Table 133.

Percentage of U.S.	Northeast	Percentage of U.S.	Central	Percentage of U.S.	West	Percentage of U.S.
51.6	695,152	21.0	665,839	20.1	241,073	7.3
50.5	77,879	20.9	74,712	20.0	32,267	8.6
36.5	19,536	33.1	11,467	19.5	6,454	10.9
36.9	7,645	26.7	7,965	27.8	2,446	8.6
64.8	19,567	11.7	28,345	17.0	10,890	6.5
43.2	1,391	23.6	1,288	21.9	667	11.3
40.5	29,740	26.3	25,647	22.7	11,810	10.5
45.6	10,966	22.8	10,303	21.4	4,882	10.2
40.6	20,078	23.9	21,688	25.8	8,168	9.7
40.6	16,663	23.8	18,273	26.0	6,703	9.6
40.8	3,415	24.4	3,415	24.4	1,465	10.4
31.9	209,631	30.7	182,106	26.6	74,071	10.8
26.0	11,225	35.6	8,382	26.6	3,738	11.8
33.6	54,571	30.5	44,810	25.1	19,306	10.8
31.7	143,835	30.3	128,914	27.2	51,027	10.8
48.0	10,179	21.5	11,260	23.8	3,185	6.7
50.8	125,150	23.5	108,516	20.3	28,710	5.4
65.7	1,749	13.3	2,250	17.0	522	4.0
57.4	6,715	13.6	11,926	24.1	2,410	4.9
55.2	1,128	20.0	1,157	20.5	246	4.3
87.8	1,698	4.9	1,800	5.2	739	2.1
53.9	150,273	17.8	179,069	21.2	59,147	7.1
61.4	27,632	13.5	37,985	18.5	13,578	6.6
67.1	23,257	10.1	41,425	18.0	11,081	0.8
40.4	57,497	25.7	56,610	25.3	19,142	8.6
47.7	16,771	21.0	17,441	21.9	7,462	9.4
35.3	2,739	34.8	1,817	23.1	529	6.8
44.5	22,377	23.2	23,791	24.7	7,355	7.6
71.7	79,706	13.5	61,052	10.3	26,726	4.5

Table R.10   Work Experience of Women by Age, 1976

			Distribution of Workers			
		Percentage	Full-Time			Part-Time
Age and Race	Number (× 1,000)	with Work Experience	50–52 Weeks	27–49 Weeks	1–26 Weeks	
16 years and over	82,059	54.5	41.1	12.3	13.0	33.6
White	71,799	54.6	40.6	12.1	12.7	34.6
Black	8,896	53.1	45.4	14.0	14.6	26.0
16–19 years	8,302	59.0	7.9	6.7	20.7	64.8
White	7,017	63.6	8.2	6.6	19.8	65.4
Black	1,139	31.3	6.1	8.7	31.1	54.2
20–24 years	9,804	75.8	36.3	16.6	19.9	26.7
White	8,348	78.5	36.9	17.0	18.7	27.3
Black	1,265	60.2	32.4	17.9	28.8	20.9
25–44 years	28,338	65.5	45.8	13.5	11.7	29.0
White	24,460	65.1	44.4	13.1	11.6	30.9
Black	3,264	68.9	55.6	15.7	11.3	17.5
45–64 years	22,647	54.3	52.4	10.8	8.0	28.8
White	20,192	54.1	52.5	10.8	8.0	28.7
Black	2,153	55.9	50.3	11.2	7.7	30.8
65 years and over	12,968	11.8	22.5	5.7	11.2	60.6
White	11,782	11.6	23.6	5.7	11.6	59.0
Black	1,076	14.0	13.4	5.5	7.7	73.3

Source: U.S. Department of Labor, Bureau of Labor Statistics, *Work Experience of the Population in 1976*. Special Labor Force Report No. 201, Tables B-7 and B-21.

Table R.11 Black Women with Work Experience in Selected Occupations by Full- and Part-Time Status, 1976

Major Occupation	Number (× 1,000)	Experience in Full-Time Jobs			Experience in Part-Time Jobs		
		50-52 Weeks	27-49 Weeks	1-26 Weeks	50-52 Weeks	27-49 Weeks	1-26 Weeks
All Occupations	4,721	45.4	14.0	14.6	9.3	5.6	11.0
Professional, technical, and kindred workers	594	69.2	12.3	7.7	2.8	3.3	4.6
Managers and administrators, except farm	120	69.4	11.8	3.8	4.3	2.8	8.0
Sales workers	122	23.8	8.2	16.0	9.1	8.9	33.9
Clerical and kindred	1,167	53.9	13.1	17.7	4.2	3.1	7.9
Operatives, except transport	755	50.2	20.0	18.5	2.9	3.7	2.7
Private household workers	465	14.2	6.1	3.0	42.3	12.0	22.4
Service workers, except private households	1,283	40.0	15.1	15.1	10.0	7.5	12.4
Farm laborers and foremen	94	5.4	3.0	41.0	3.7	5.0	41.9

Source: U.S. Department of Labor, Bureau of Labor Statistics, *Work Experience of the Population in 1976.* Special Labor Force Report No. 201, Table B-6.

Appendix A

Table R.12 Median Years of School Completed by Women in the
Employed Civilian Labor Force by Occupation Group, Selected Years

	March 1978	March 1975	March 1970	March 1965	March 1959
All occupation groups					
Black	12.4	12.4	12.1	11.2	9.4
White	12.6	12.6	12.5	12.4	12.3
Professional and managerial					
Black	16.0	16.4	16.3	16.3	15.6
White	15.7	16.8	15.4	14.8	14.0
Clerical and sales workers					
Black	12.7	12.7	12.6	12.6	12.5
White	12.6	12.6	12.5	12.5	12.4
Blue collar workers					
Black	12.0	12.1	11.6	10.6	9.5
White	12.1	11.8	11.0	10.2	9.8
Service workers					
Black	11.3	11.0	10.2	9.7	8.6
White	12.2	12.1	12.0	11.1	10.0
Private household					
Black	9.6	9.2	8.7	8.9	7.8
White	11.2	11.0	9.9	8.9	8.7
Other service workers					
Black	12.0	11.7	11.2	10.7	10.0
White	12.3	12.2	12.1	11.6	10.6

Source: U.S. Department of Labor, Employment and Training Administration, *Employment and Training Report of the President*, 1979, pp. 253–254.

Table R.13 Black Women Government Workers by Occupation, 1970

Occupation	Total Government	Percentage of Total	Federal	State	Local
Total	806,674	100.0	229,231	182,377	395,066
Professional, technical, kindred	248,669	30.8	29,836	53,617	165,216
Librarians	5,382		526	1,357	3,499
Registered nurses	19,570		3,848	5,533	10,189
Dietitians	3,077		822	909	1,346
Therapists	1,379		198	562	619
Social workers	18,928		3,302	4,487	11,139
Teachers	153,119		7,954	29,981	115,184
College	5,206		344	3,751	1,111
Elementary and preschool	109,596		6,276	18,566	84,754
Secondary	35,497		741	6,772	27,984
Others	2,820		593	892	1,335
All others	47,214		13,186	10,788	23,240
Managers and administrators (except farm)	16,534	2.0	5,151	2,713	8,670
School administrators	4,076		292	819	2,965
All others	12,458		4,859	1,894	5,705
Sales workers	3,506	0.4	1,536	618	1,352
Clerical and kindred	266,786	33.1	134,053	44,361	88,372
Bookkeepers	7,486		3,714	1,139	2,633
Cashiers	4,256		1,432	856	1,968
File clerks	15,965		8,449	2,877	4,639
Library attendants	5,132		610	1,384	3,138

Office machine operators	11,973		7,421	2,018	2,534
Keypunch operators	8,408		5,174	1,398	1,836
Postal clerks	28,595		28,595	. . . .	. . . .
Receptionists	4,666		1,240	1,369	2,057
Secretaries	34,175		13,671	8,030	12,474
Statistical clerks	5,555		3,106	666	1,783
Stenographers	3,638		1,458	915	1,265
Teachers' aides	21,159		2,891	3,296	14,972
Typists	42,700		18,704	9,078	14,918
Others	81,486		42,762	12,733	25,991
Craftsmen and kindred workers	5,490	0.7	2,572	996	1,922
Operatives, except transport	26,274	3.3	12,901	5,442	7,931
Transport equipment operatives	4,515	0.6	530	801	3,184
Laborers, except farm	6,854	0.8	4,105	791	1,958
Farm workers	529	0.1	232	137	160
Service workers, except private household	227,517	28.2	38,315	72,901	116,301
Cleaning service workers	46,900		9,146	13,679	24,075
Food service workers	57,579		9,337	16,580	31,662
Health service workers	74,169		11,057	30,355	32,757
Nursing aides	51,430		6,802	23,536	21,092
Practical nurses	15,453		2,696	4,552	8,205
Personal service workers	20,264		4,138	5,979	10,147
Child care workers	8,240		1,831	3,037	3,372
Others	28,605		4,637	6,308	17,660

Source: U.S. Bureau of the Census, Census of Population: 1970. Subject Report, Final Report PC(2)-7D, *Government Workers*, Table 2.

Table R.14 Wives' Contribution to Nonfarm Family Income, Selected Years

Contribution	1966 White	1966 Black	1969 White	1969 Black	1972 White	1972 Black	1976 White	1976 Black
Less than 5.0%	22.2	19.5	11.3	7.2	10.6	6.7	13.5	5.8
5.0 –9.9%	8.7	8.2	10.0	8.5	9.8	6.6	9.1	6.0
10.0–19.9%	14.3	15.1	17.4	14.6	18.1	15.8	17.1	12.6
20.0–29.9%	15.8	15.8	18.3	18.4	18.5	17.4	18.3	17.9
30.0–39.9%	16.9	16.3	18.6	18.7	18.5	19.7	17.2	20.1
40.0–49.9%	12.1	12.8	13.0	17.3	13.0	17.9	13.4	18.7
50.0–74.9%	7.7	9.9	9.3	12.5	9.0	12.8	9.0	15.6
75.0% and over	2.2	2.2	2.2	2.9	2.3	3.2	2.3	3.2
Median percentage	23.0	24.5	26.2	30.8	26.1	31.8	25.6	33.8

Sources: U.S. Department of Labor, Bureau of Labor Statistics, *Marital and Family Characteristics of the Labor Force, March 1977*, Special Labor Force Report No. 216, Table A, pp. 42–43.

U.S. Department of Labor, Bureau of Labor Statistics, *Marital and Family Characteristics of the Labor Force, March 1973*, Special Labor Force Report No. 164, p. 29.

U.S. Department of Labor, Bureau of Labor Statistics, *Marital and Family Characteristics of Workers, March 1970*, Special Labor Force Report No. 164, p. 29.

U.S. Department of Labor, Bureau of Labor Statistics, *Marital and Family Characteristics of Workers, March 1967*, Special Labor Force Report No. 94, p. A-23.

Note: This table only refers to families where the husband is present. Wives' contribution refers to wives' earnings.

Table R.15 Median Family Income in 1974 by Earning Status of
Husband and Wife, by Age and Race of Husband

		Husband-Wife Families	
Age of Husband	All Families	Husband Only Earner	Husband and Wife Both Earners
White			
Under 35 years	$12,152	$12,031	$13,639
14–24 years	9,151	7,759	10,626
25–34 years	13,294	12,789	15,228
35–44 years	15,850	14,463	18,192
45–54 years	17,059	13,556	19,771
55–64 years	14,137	12,694	18,157
65 years and over	7,518	8,350	12,763
Total	13,271	12,541	16,553
Black			
Under 35 years	$ 7,151	$ 8,096	$12,783
14–24 years	4,790	6,121	8,989
25–34 years	8,621	9,093	14,193
35–44 years	9,045	9,777	13,891
45–54 years	10,068	10,280	15,411
55–64 years	8,218	7,697	11,939
65 years and over	4,874	. . . . .[a]	. . . . .[a]
Total	7,807	8,555	13,316
Black/White Income Ratio			
Under 35 years	58.8%	67.3%	93.7%
14–24 years	52.3	78.9	84.6
25–34 years	64.8	71.1	93.2
35–44 years	57.1	67.6	76.4
45–54 years	59.0	75.8	77.9
55–64 years	58.1	60.6	65.8
65 years and over	64.8		
Total	58.8	68.2	80.4

Source: U.S. Bureau of the Census, Current Population Reports,
Series P-60, No. 101, *Money Income in 1974 of Families and Persons
in the U.S.*, Table 74.

a. Base less than 75,000.

Appendix B

The federal government routinely publishes a number of statistical series that provide detailed information on the labor market status of workers. A monthly household survey conducted by the Bureau of the Census for the Bureau of Labor Statistics, the Current Population Survey (CPS), provides information on employment and unemployment by age, sex, race, marital and household status, occupational and industry groups. In March of each year, supplementary questions are included in the CPS on the work experience of the population during the preceding year, on the marital and family characteristics of workers, and on the income of families and individuals. Four reports are based on the expanded March surveys: *Work Experience of the Population, Marital and Family Characteristics of the Labor Force, Money Income of Families and Persons in the United States,* and *Characteristics of the Population Below the Poverty Level.*

The 1970 decennial census volumes, *Negro Population and Employment Status and Work Experience, Occupational Characteristics,* and *Earnings by Occupation and Income,* provide a wealth of detailed information on black women workers by age, marital status, occupation, industry, educational attainment, presence of children, geographic location, and work experience. Black women workers may be compared in this manner with other women workers, with black and white males, and with specific subsets of black women. Although these census series may be used for simple comparisons, they are limited. Data from the 1/1000 sample of households in the census (public use data tapes) are used for more sophisticated analysis of labor force participation.

Other annual and monthly series used are *Employment and Training Report of the President* (annually), *Employment and Earnings* (monthly), and *Monthly Labor Review* (monthly). In 1976 a large special *Survey of Income and Education* (SIE) of 151,000 households was conducted for the Department of Health, Education, and Welfare. Several publications using SIE data have been released in the *Current Population Reports*.

Notes

Chapter 1

1

Michael C. Barth, et al., *Toward an Effective Income Support System: Problems, Prospects and Choices* (Madison: Institute for Research on Poverty, University of Wisconsin, 1974), p. 10.

2

Bennett Harrison, *Labor Market Structure and the Relationship Between Work and Welfare,* Working Paper No. 50, Joint Center for Urban Studies of MIT and Harvard University, May 1978, pp. 26–27.

3

U.S. Department of Labor, Bureau of Labor Statistics, *Marital and Family Characteristics of Workers in March 1977,* Special Labor Force Report 216, Table P., p. A48.

4

Solomon Polacheck, "Differences in Expected Post-School Investment as a Determinant of Market Differentials," *Women, Minorities, and Employment Discrimination,* ed. Phyllis A. Wallace and Annette LaMond (Lexington, Mass.: Lexington Books, 1977); and George E. Johnson and Frank P. Stafford, "The Earnings and Promotion of Women Faculty," *The American Economic Review, vol. LXIV, no. 6, December 1974, pp. 888–903.*

5

Herbert S. Parnes, "Labor Force Participation and Labor Mobility," *A Review of Industrial Relations Research,* vol. I (Madison, Wisc.: Industrial Relations Research Association, 1970), p. 33.

6

Dale L. Hiestand, *Economic Growth and Employment Opportunities for Minorities* (New York: Columbia University Press, 1964), p. 53.

7

Ibid., p. 44.

8

Bernard E. Anderson and Phyllis A. Wallace, "Public Policy and Black Economic Progress: A Review of the Evidence," *American Economic Review,* Papers and Proceedings 65 (May 1975), pp. 47–52.

Chapter 2

1

Jacob Mincer, "Labor Force Participation of Married Women: A Study of Labor Supply," *Aspects of Labor Economics,* National Bureau of Economic Research, (Princeton, N.J.: Princeton University Press, 1962); Gary Becker, "A Theory of the Allocation of Time," *Economic Journal* 75 (Sept. 1965), pp. 493–517; Arleen Leibowitz, "Education and the Allocation of Women's Time," *Education, Income and Human Behavior,* ed. Juster F. Thomas (New York: McGraw-Hill Book Company, 1975), pp. 171–197.

2

Mincer, "Labor Force Participation of Married Women," pp. 81–82.

3

Glen Cain, *Married Women in the Labor Force* (Chicago: University of Chicago Press, 1966).

4

Ibid., pp. 119–120.

5

Ibid.

6

Glen Cain and Martin Dooley, "Estimation of a Model of Labor Supply, Fertility, and Wages of Married Women," *Journal of Political Economy,* vol. 84, no. 4 (August 1976), p. S195.

7

William G. Bowen and T. Aldrich Finegan, *The Economics of Labor Force Participation* (Princeton, N.J.: Princeton University Press, 1969), p. 90.

8

Ibid., pp. 91–93.

9

Ibid., passim.

10

Ibid., p. 253.

11

Ibid., pp. 416–418.

12

Duran Bell, "Why Participation Rates of Black and White Wives Differ," *The Journal of Human Resources* IX (1974), p. 466.

13

Ibid., p. 471

14

Ibid., pp. 472–474.

15

Ibid., p. 477.

16

Dual Careers: A Longitudinal Study of Labor Market Experience of Women. Vol. 1 (by John R. Shea, et al.), Center for Human Resource Research, The Ohio State University, 1970. Vol. 2 (by John R. Shea, et al.), U.S. Government Printing Office, 1973. Vol. 3 (by Carol Jusenius and Richard L. Shortlidge, Jr.), Center for Human Resource Research, The Ohio State University, 1975. Vol. 4 (by Herbert S. Parnes, et al.), Center for Human Resource Research, The Ohio State University, 1975.

Just recently the U.S. Department of Labor has published the *Dual Careers* series in a monograph series: *Dual Careers: A Longitudinal Study of Labor Market Experience of Women,* Manpower Research Monograph 21.

17

Dual Careers,

18

Frank L. Mott, "The NLS Mature Women's Cohort: A Socioeconomic Overview," *Women's Changing Roles at Home and on the Job,* National Commission for Manpower Policy Special Report No. 26, Washington, D. C. pp. 28–29.

19

Dual Careers, vol. 4 (by Herbert S. Parnes, et al.), pp. 186–187.

20

Barbara A. Jones, "The Contribution of Black Women to the Incomes of Black Families: An Analysis of the Labor Force," Ph.D. dissertation, 1973.

21

Orley Ashenfelter, and James Heckman, "The Estimation of Income and Substitution Effects in a Model of Family Labor Supply," *Econometrica* 42 (January 1974), pp. 73–85.

22

Glenn Loury, "A Dynamic Theory of Racial Income Differences" *Women, Minorities, and Employment Discrimination,* eds. Phyllis A.

Wallace and Annette LaMond (Lexington, Mass.: Lexington Books, 1977) pp. 153–186.

Chapter 3

1

Richard B. Freeman, *Black Elites* (New York: McGraw Hill Book Company, 1976), pp. 5–10; Duran Bell, *The Economic Impact of the Social Legislation of the 1960's on Blacks in the Labor Market,* The RAND Corporation, P-5202, March 1974, pp. 7–8.

2

Bell, *The Economic Impact of the Social Legislation,* p. 7.

3

Julianne Malveaux, "Unemployment Differentials by Race and Occupation," Ph.D. dissertation, Massachusetts Institute of Technology, 1980.

4

Dual Careers: A Longitudinal Study of Labor Market Experience of Women. Vol. 1 (by John R. Shea, et al.), Center for Human Resource Research, The Ohio State University, 1970, p. 108.

5

Dual Careers, vol. 1 (by Herbert S. Parnes, et al.), pp. 72–82.

6

Ibid., p. 82.

7

Ibid., p. 85.

8

Stuart Garfinkle, "Occupations of Women and Black Workers," *The Monthly Labor Review,* vol. 98, no. 11 (Nov. 1975), p. 31.

9

Carol Leon and Robert W. Bednarzik, "A Profile of Women On Part-Time Schedules," *Monthly Labor Review,* vol. 101, no. 10 (Oct. 1978), p. 7.

10

Duran Bell, "Why Participation Rates of Black and White Wives Differ," *The Journal of Human Resources,* vol. IX, no. 4, p. 474.

11

Dual Careers, vol. 1 (by John R. Shea, et al.), p. 129.

12

William G. Bowen and Aldrich T. Finegan, *The Economics of Labor Force Participation,* (Princeton, N.J.: Princeton University Press, 1969), p. 115.

13

Ibid., pp. 122–127.

14

Ibid., pp. 118–122.

15

Jones, "The Contribution of Black Women to the Incomes of Black Families," p. 44.

16

Patricia Gurin and Carolyn Gaylord, "Educational and Occupational Goals of Men and Women at Black Colleges," *Monthly Labor Review,* vol. 99, no. 6 (June 1976), p. 10–16.

17

Ibid.

18

Otis Dudley Duncan, "Inheritance of Poverty or Inheritance of Race," *On Understanding Poverty,* ed. Daniel P. Moynihan, (New York: Basic Books, Inc., 1968).

19

Bowen and Finegan, *The Economics of Labor Force Participation,* p. 100.

20

Jones, "The Contribution of Black Women to the Incomes of Black Families," p. 57.

21

Allyson Sherman Grossman, *Children of Working Mothers, March 1976,* Special Labor Force Report, No. 205, U.S. Department of Labor, Bureau of Labor Statistics, Washington, D.C.

22

Myra R. Strober, "Economic Aspects of Child Care," *American Women Workers in a Full Employment Economy,* Joint Economic Committee, Congress of the United States, Washington, D.C., 1971.

Chapter 4

1

Peter B. Doeringer and Michael J. Piore, *Internal Labor Markets and Manpower Analysis* (Lexington, Mass.: D. C. Heath, 1971), p. 165.

2

Michael L. Wachter, "Primary and Secondary Labor Markets: A Critique of the Dual Approach," *Brookings Papers on Economic Activity* 3 (1974), p. 653.

3

Bennett Harrison and Andrew Sum, "The Theory of 'Dual' or 'Segmented' Labor Markets: A Stock-Taking on the State of the Art," manuscript, Dec. 1978, p. 15. To be published in the *Journal of Economic Issues*, 1979–1980.

4

Annette LaMond, "Economic Theories of Employment Discrimination," *Women, Minorities, and Employment Discrimination*, eds. Phyllis A. Wallace and Annette LaMond (Lexington, Mass.: Lexington Books, 1977).

5

Glen Cain, "The Challenge of Segmented Labor Market Theories to Orthodox Theory: A Survey," *Journal of Economic Literature*, vol. XIV, no. 4 (December 1976), p. 1219.

6

Charles Perry, et al., *The Impact of Government Manpower Programs*, (Philadelphia, Penn.: University of Pennsylvania Press, 1975), p. 141.

7

Ibid., p. 142.

8

Ibid., pp. 141–142.

9

Ibid., p. 142.

10

Nicholas Kiefer, "The Economic Benefits from Manpower Training Programs," *Cost Effectiveness Analysis of Four Categorical Employment and Training Programs: MDTA, JOBS, Job Corps, and the Neighborhood Youth Corps Out of School*, eds. Gordon P. Goodfellow and Ernst Stormsdorfer, U.S. Department of Labor, 1977.

11

Ibid., p. 181.

12

Emergency Jobs Program, Extension Act of 1976, Public Law 94-444; and The Comprehensive Employment and Training Amendments of 1978 (CETA Reauthorization Act), Public Law 95-524.

13

Stuart Garfinkle, "The Outcome of a Spell of Unemployment," *The Monthly Labor Review,* vol. 100, no. 1, p. 56.

14

Curtis Gilroy, *Unemployment in Recessions: Women and Black Workers,* U.S. Department of Labor, April 1977; and Curtis Gilroy, "Black and White Unemployment: The Dynamics of the Differential," *The Monthly Labor Review,* vol. 97, no. 2 (February 1974), p. 48.

15

Nancy Barrett and Richard Morgenstern, "Why Do Blacks and Women Have High Unemployment Rates?" *The Journal of Human Resources,* vol. IX, no. 4, p. 458.

16

Barbara R. Bergmann, "Studying Black-White Differences in the Context of a Microsimulation of the Labor Market," *Patterns of Racial Discrimination,* eds. von Furstenberg et al. (Lexington, Mass.: Lexington Books, 1974).

17

Charles Holt, "Modeling a Segmented Labor Market," *Women, Minorities, and Employment Discrimination,* eds. Phyllis A. Wallace and Annette LaMond (Lexington, Mass.: Lexington Books, 1977); and Ralph E. Smith, "The Impact of Macroeconomic Conditions on Employment Opportunities for Women," *Achieving the Goals of the Employment Act of 1946,* paper no. 6, Joint Economic Committee, Congress of the United States, 1977.

18

National Commission on Employment and Unemployment Statistics, *Counting the Labor Force,* Washington, D.C., Sept. 1979.

19

Larry Sawers, "Urban Poverty and Labor Force Participation," *The American Economic Review,* vol. LXII, no. 3, (June 1973), p. 420.

20

Bowen and Finegan, *The Economics of Labor Force Participation* (Princeton, N.J.: Princeton University Press, 1969), p. 512.

21
Glen Cain, "Unemployment and Labor Force Participation of Secondary Workers," *Industrial Labor Relations Review,* 20 (January 1967), pp. 275–297.

22
Orley Ashenfelter, "Minority Employment Patterns, 1966," monograph, Princeton, N.J., 1968, p. 1.

23
Orley Ashenfelter and James Heckman, "Analysis of Equal Employment Opportunities for Minorities and Women, 1966–70," Equal Employment Opportunity Commission, Washington, D.C., 1973, p. 6.

24
Barbara Reagan, "Comments on Ashenfelter and Heckman Paper," MIT Research Workshop on Equal Employment Opportunity, January 1974, pp. 3–4.

25
Ray Marshall and Virgil L. Christian, ed., *Employment of Blacks in the South,* (Austin: University of Texas Press, 1978), pp. 185–199.

26
Payne v. Travenol Laboratories, 12 FEP Cases 770, February 1976.

27
Tippell v. Liggett and Myers Tobacco Co., 11 FEP Cases 1307, October 1975.

28
Final Report of *Equal Employment Opportunity Commission et al. v. AT & T et al.,* January 17, 1969, Civil Action 73–149, Eastern District of Penna.

29
U.S. Civil Service Commission, *Equal Employment Opportunity Statistics,* Washington, D. C., Nov. 1977, p. 2.

30
Lester Thurow, "The Indirect Incidence of Government Expenditures," unpublished paper, January 1979.

31
William Barnes, "Target Groups," *CETA: An Analysis of the Issues,* Special Report no. 23, National Commission for Manpower Policy, May 1978, p. 83.

Chapter 5

1

Sar Levitan, et al., *Still A Dream* (Cambridge, Mass.: Harvard University Press, 1975), pp. 60–61.

2

Using data from U.S. Bureau of the Census, Census of Population, 1970, Subject Reports, Final Report PC (2)-8B, *Earnings by Occupation and Education,* we calculate a mean earnings that black women would receive if they were distributed in job categories by education the same as white women (i.e., the fraction of black women in each job-education category) of $5,186. The mean earnings of white women 25–34 years of age is $5,308. Therefore, if black women had the same distribution as white women, they would still receive less earnings.

3

Dual Careers: A Longitudinal Study of Labor Market Experience of Women. Vol. 3 (by Carol Jusenius and Richard L. Shortlidge, Jr.), Center for Human Resource Research, The Ohio State University, 1975.

4

Based on information available to author from friends, family, and other older black public school teachers.

5

Paula Hudis, "Commitment to Work and Wages: Earnings Differences of Black and White Women," *Sociology of Work and Occupations,* vol. 4, no. 2 (May 1977), p. 137.

6

Ronald N. Oaxaca, "The Persistence of Male-Female Earnings Differentials," ed. by F. Thomas Juster, *The Distribution of Economic Well-Being,* (Cambridge, Mass.: Ballinger Publishing Company, 1977), pp. 303–344.

7

Nancy D. Ruggles and Richard Ruggles, "The Anatomy of Earnings Behavior," ed. by F. Thomas Juster, *The Distribution of Economic Well-Being,* (Cambridge, Mass.: Ballinger Publishing Company, 1977), pp. 115–158.

8

Ibid., p. 133, 141, 152.

9
Nancy Smith Barrett, "Comments On the Anatomy of Earnings Behavior," ed. by F. Thomas Juster, *The Distribution of Economic Well-Being*, (Cambridge, Mass.: Ballinger Publishing Company, 1977), pp. 161–162.

10
U.S. Department of Commerce, U.S. Bureau of the Census, "Money Income in 1976 of Families and Persons in the United States," *Current Population Reports*, Series P-60, No. 114, Table 45, 1978.

11
U.S. Department of Labor, Bureau of Labor Statistics, *Marital and Family Characteristics of Workers*, Special Report 216, Table P, March 1977.

12
U.S. Department of Commerce, U.S. Bureau of the Census, "Money Income in 1974 of Families and Persons in the United States," *Current Population Reports*, Series P-60, No. 101, Table 72, 1976.

13
Joan Haworth, "Changes in the Relative Economic Status of Women From 1960–1970," Office of Economic Research, Economic Development Administration, U.S. Department of Commerce, Washington, D.C., 1973.

Chapter 6

1
Paula M. Hudis, "Commitment to Work and Wages: Earnings Differences of Black and White Women," *Sociology of Work and Occupations*, vol. 4, no. 2 (May 1977), pp. 125–126.

2
Phyllis A. Wallace, *Pathways to Work: Unemployment Among Black Teenage Females*, (Lexington, Mass.: Lexington Books, 1974).

3
Hylan G. Lewis, et al., *Improving Employment Opportunities for Female Black Teenagers in New York City*, R & D Monograph 47, U.S. Department of Labor, 1977.

4
Herbert Parnes, et al., *Years for Decision: A Longitudinal Study of the Education and Labor Market Experience of Young Women*, Center

for Human Resource Research, The Ohio State University, vol. I-IV, 1971, 1973, 1974, and 1978. Published also as Manpower Research Monograph 24, U.S. Department of Labor.

5

Ibid., vol. I, pp. 49, 56, 98.

6

Beverly L. Johnson, "Women Who Head Families, 1970-1977: Their Numbers Rose, Income Lagged," *Monthly Labor Review,* vol. 101, no. 2, (February 1978), pp. 32-37.

7

Ibid., p. 36.

8

Heather L. Ross and Isabel V. Sawhill, *Time of Transition: The Growth of Families Headed by Women,* Urban Institute, Washington, D.C., 1975.

9

Mary Fish, *Income Inequality and Employment,* R & D Monograph 66, U.S. Department of Labor, 1978.

10

Bennett Harrison, "Labor Market Structure and the Relationship Between Work and Welfare," unpublished manuscript, p. 38.

11

Richard B. Freeman, "Black Economic Progress After 1964: Who Has Gained and Why?" *National Bureau of Economic Research Working Paper* no. 282, Nov. 1978; Robert E. Hall and Richard A. Kasten, "The Relative Occupational Success of Blacks and Whites," *Brookings Papers on Economic Activity* 3 (1973), pp. 781-795.

12

"Better Jobs and Income Act," Draft Bill, Department of Health, Education, and Welfare, August 6, 1977.

13

"Proposal for Welfare Reform," Work and Training Opportunities Act of 1979 and the Social Welfare Reform Amendments of 1979, May 23, 1979.

14

Alicia H. Munnell, "The Economic Experience of Blacks: 1964-1974," *New England Economic Review,* Federal Reserve Bank of Boston, Jan.-Feb. 1978, pp. 12-15.

15
"Private Household Workers," U.S. Department of Labor, Employment Standards Administration, 1974.

16
M. K. Trimble, *Final Report of the National Pilot Program on Household Employment* (Washington, D.C.: NTIS, 1971).

17
"Private Household Workers."

18
David Chaplin, "Upward Mobility for Private Household Workers," prepared for a Workshop on Research Needed to Improve the Employment and Employability of Women, U.S. Department of Labor, June 1974, p. 2.

19
J. Miller and L. Ferman, *Welfare Careers and Low Wage Employment,* Institute of Labor and Industrial Relations, University of Michigan, December 1972, p. 2.

20
Chaplin, "Upward Mobility for Private Household Workers," p. 7.

21
Ibid., p. 2.

22
"Private Household Workers," p. 27.

23
David Chaplin, "Domestic Service and the Rationalization of Household Economy," Department of Sociology, University of Wisconsin, 1968.

24
Lillian Pettengill, *Toilers of the Home* (New York: Doubleday, Page and Co., 1903.) Cited in M. K. Trimble, *Final Report of the National Pilot Program on Household Employment* (Washington, D.C.: National Technical Information Service, 1971), p. 15.

25
National Committee on Household Employment, *Final Report of the Experimental and Demonstration Projects,* (Washington, D.C.: National Technical Information Service, 1971), p. 44.

26
Ibid.

27

M. K. Trimble, *Final Report of the National Pilot Program on Household Employment,* pp. 2–7.

28

"Thirteen Year Olds Trapped in Domestic Racket," *Long Island Journal,* November 16, 1955.

29

Career Ladders and Lattices in Home Economics and Related Areas: Possibilities of Upgrading Household Employment, American Home Economics Association, 1971.

30

Jack Barbash, "The Emergence of Urban Low-Wage Unionism," *Industrial Relations Research Association Series,* April 1974, p. 275.

31

Ibid.; and Chaplin, "Domestic Service and the Rationalization of Household Economy," pp. 18–19.

32

David Chaplin, "Upward Mobility for Private Household Workers."

33

Harold Wool, *The Labor Supply for Lower-Level Occupations* (New York: Praeger Publishers, 1976).

34

J. Peter Mantilla, "Labor Supply of Household Maids," *Labor Supply for Lower-Level Occupations,* ed. Harold Wool, Final Report. September 1975.

Chapter 7

1

Charles T. Stewart, Jr., *Low-Wage Workers in an Affluent Society* (Nelson Hall, 1974). Cited in U.S. Department of Labor, *Income, Inequality and Employment,* R & D Monograph 66, Washington, D.C., 1978.

2

Frank S. Levy, "How Big Is The American Underclass?" in *The Income Dynamics of the Poor,* by Frank S. Levy, Clair Vickery, and Michael Wiseman (Berkeley, California: Institute of Business and Economic Research, University of California, January 1977).

3
Schooling and Work Among Youths from Low Income Households: A Baseline Report from the Entitlement Demonstration, Manpower Demonstration Research Corporation, May 1979.

4
A Model of the Effect of Income Maintenance on Rates of Marital Dissolution: Evidence from the Seattle and Denver Income Maintenance Experiments, Research Memorandum 44, Stanford Research Institute, Center for the Study of Welfare Policy, February 1979.

5
Phyllis A. Wallace, *Affirmative Action and Increased Labor Force Participation of Women,* Sloan School Working Paper No. 1060-79, April 1979.

Bibliography

Almquist, Elizabeth M. "Untangling the Effects of Race and Sex: The Disadvantaged Status of Black Women." *Social Science Quarterly* 56 (June 1975): 129–142.

American Home Economics Association. *Career Ladders and Lattices in Home Economics and Related Areas: Possibilities for Upgrading Household Employment, 1.* Washington, D.C.: American Home Economics Association, 1971.

Anderson, Bernard E., and Wallace, Phyllis A. "Public Policy and Black Economic Progress: A Review of the Evidence." *American Economic Review*, Papers and Proceedings 65 (May 1975): 47–52.

Ash, Philip. "Job Satisfaction Differences Among Women of Different Ethnic Groups." *Journal of Vocational Behavior* 2 (1972): 495–507.

Ashenfelter, Orley. "Changes in Labor Market Discrimination Over Time." *Journal of Human Resources* 5 (Fall 1970): 403–430.

Ashenfelter, Orley. *Minority Employment Patterns, 1966.* Industrial Relations Section, Princeton University, 1968.

Ashenfelter, Orley, and Heckman, James. "Measuring the Effect of an Antidiscrimination Program." Working Paper No. 52, Industrial Relations Section, Princeton University, 1974.

Barbash, Jack. "The Emergence of Urban Low-Wage Unionism." *Proceedings of Twenty-Sixth Annual Winter Meeting,* Industrial Relations Research Association Series, Winter 1973, pp. 275–284.

Barnes, William. "Target Groups." *CETA: An Analysis of the Issues.* Special Report No. 23, National Commission for Manpower Policy, May 1978.

Barrett, Nancy, and Morgenstern, Richard. "Why Do Blacks Have High Unemployment Rates?" *The Journal of Human Resources* 9 (Fall 1974): 452–464.

Barth, Michael C., et al. *Towards an Effective Income Support: Problems, Prospects, Choices.* Madison Institute for Research on Poverty, 1974.

Beal, Frances M. "Double Jeopardy: To Be Black and Female." *New Generation* 51 (Fall 1969).

Becker, Gary. "A Theory of the Allocation of Time." *Economic Journal* 75 (Sept. 1965): 493–517.

Bell, Duran, Jr. "The Economic Basis of Employee Discrimination." *Patterns of Racial Discrimination*, vol. 2, ed. George M. von Furstenberg et al., pp. 121-136. Lexington, Mass.: Lexington Books, 1974.

Bell, Duran, Jr. *The Economic Impact of the Social Legislation of the 1960's on Blacks in the Labor Market.* RAND p-5202, March 1974.

Bell, Duran, Jr. "Occupational Discrimination As A Source of Income Differences: Lessons of the 1960's." *American Economic Review*, Proceedings and Papers 62 (May 1972): 363-372.

Bell, Duran, Jr. "Why Participation Rates of Black and White Wives Differ." *The Journal of Human Resources* 9 (Fall 1974): 465-479.

Bergmann, Barbara R. "Studying Black-White Differences in the Context of a Microsimulation of the Labor Market." *Patterns of Racial Discrimination*, vol. 2, ed. George M. von Furstenberg et al., pp. 27-32. Lexington, Mass.: Lexington Books, 1974.

Bergmann, Barbara. "The Effect On White Incomes Of Discrimination in Employment." *The Journal of Political Economy* 79 (March/April 1971): 294-313.

Bergmann, Barbara. "Occupational Segregation, Wages and Profits When Employers Discriminate By Race Or Sex." Project on the Economics of Discrimination, University of Maryland, October 1970.

Bergmann, Barbara R., and Lyle, Jerolyn R. "The Occupational Standing of Negroes by Areas and Industries." *The Journal of Human Resources* 6 (Fall 1971): 411-433.

Blau, Peter M., and Duncan, Otis D. *The American Occupational Structure.* New York: John Wiley and Sons, Inc., 1967.

Blood, Kathryn. *Negro Women War Workers.* Bulletin No. 205. Washington, D.C.: U.S. Department of Labor, Women's Bureau, 1945.

Bock, E. Wilbur. "Farmer's Daughter Effect: The Case of the Negro Female Professionals." *Phylon* 30 (Spring 1959): 17-26.

Bowen, William G., and Finegan, T. Aldrich. *The Economics of Labor Force Participation.* Princeton, N.J.: Princeton University Press, 1969.

Bressler, Tobia, and Nampeo, McKenney. "Negro Women in the United States." Paper presented at Population Association of America, Boston, Massachusetts, April 18-20, 1968.

Brimmer, Andrew F. *The Economic Position of Black Americans: 1976.* Special Report No. 9. Washington, D.C.: National Commission for Manpower Policy, 1976.

Brimmer, Andrew F. "Employment and Income in the Black Community, Trends and Outlook." Unpublished manuscript, University of California at Los Angeles, 1973.

Brimmer, Andrew F. "Widening Horizons: Prospects for Black Employment." *Labor Law Journal* 25 (June 1974): 323–335.

Bryant, Willa C. "Discrimination Against Women in General: Black Southern Women in Particular." *Civil Rights Digest* 4 (Summer 1971): 10–11.

Byron, William. "The Applicability of the Job Bank Concept to the Washington, D.C., Market for Domestic Day Workers." Ph.D. dissertation, University of Maryland, 1968.

Cade, Toni, ed. *The Black Woman: An Anthology.* New York: Signet, 1970.

Cain, Glen. *Married Women in the Labor Force: An Economic Analysis.* Chicago: University of Chicago Press, 1966.

Cain, Glen, "Unemployment and the Labor Force Participation of Secondary Workers." *Industrial and Labor Relations Review* 20 (Jan. 1967): 375–397.

Cain, Glen. "The Challenges of Segmented Labor Market Theories to Orthodox Theory: A Survey." *Journal of Economic Literature,* vol. XIV, no. 4 (Dec. 1976).

Cain, Glen, and Dooley, Martin D. "Estimation of a Model of Labor Supply, Fertility, and Wages of Married Women." *Journal of Political Economy* 84 (1976): 179–199.

Chaplin, David. "Upward Mobility for Private Household Workers." Prepared for a Workshop on Research Needed to Improve the Employment and Employability of Women, U.S. Department of Labor, June 1974.

Cohen, Malcolm S.; Rem, Samuel A.; and Lerman, Robert. *A Model of Labor Supply.* BLS Staff Paper 4. Washington, D.C.: Bureau of Labor Statistics, 1970.

Cowhig, James D. "Characteristics of Families Headed by Women, March 1968." *Welfare in Review* 8 (January/February 1970): 16–20.

Dawson, A. H. *Improving the Status of Household-Employment: A Handbook for Community Action.* Washington, D.C.: National Committee on Household Employment, October 1969.

Ditmore, Jack, and Prosser, W. R. "A Study of Day Care's Effect on the Labor Force Participation of Low-Income Mothers." Office of Economic Opportunity, June 1973.

Doeringer, Peter B., and Piore, Michael. *Internal Labor Markets and Manpower Analysis.* Lexington, Mass.: D. C. Heath, 1971.

Dual Careers: A Longitudinal Study of Labor Market Experience of Women. Vol. 1 (by John R. Shea, et al.), Center for Human Resource Research, The Ohio State University, 1970. Vol. 2 (by John R. Shea, et al.), U.S. Government Printing Office, 1973. Vol. 3 (by Carol Jusenius and Richard L. Shortlidge, Jr.), Center for Human Resource Research, The Ohio State University, 1975. Vol. 4 (by Herbert S. Parnes, et al.), Center for Human Resource Research, The Ohio State University, 1975. (See also U.S. Department of Labor.)

Dumas, Rhetaugh G. "Dilemmas of Black Females in Leadership." *Journal of Personality and Social Systems,* vol. 2, no. 1, pp. 3–14.

Duncan, Greg J., and Morgan, James, eds. *Five Thousand American Families,* vol VI. Survey Research Center, Institute for Social Research, University of Michigan, 1978.

Duncan, Otis Dudley. "Inheritance of Poverty or Inheritance of Race." *On Understanding Poverty,* ed. Daniel P. Moynihan. New York: Basic Books, 1969.

Durbin, Elizabeth. "Work and Welfare: The Case of Aid to Families with Dependent Children." *The Journal of Human Resources,* 8 (Supplement 1973): 103–125.

Epstein, Cynthia Fuchs. "Positive Effects of the Multiple Negative: Explaining the Success of Black Professional Women." *American Journal of Sociology* 78 (January 1973): 912–935.

Ferman, Louis A., and Miller, Joe A. "Welfare Careers and Low Wage Employment." Institute of Labor and Industrial Relations, University of Michigan-Wayne State University, 1972.

Fichter, Joseph H. "Career Expectations of Negro Women Graduates." (Report on 1964 study NIH-Dol-NSF). *Monthly Labor Review* 90 (Nov. 1967): 36–42.

Fichter, Joseph H. *Graduates of Predominantly Negro Colleges (Class of 1964).* Washington, D.C.: U.S. Government Printing Office, 1967.

Fields, Judith. "A Comparison of Intercity Differences in Labor Force Participation Rates of Married Women in 1970 with 1940, 1950 and 1960." *Journal of Human Resources* 2 (Fall 1976): 568–577.

Flanagan, Robert J. "Labor Force Experience, Job Turnover, and Racial Wage Differentials." *Review of Economics and Statistics,* Nov. 1974.

Freedman, Marcia. *Labor Markets: Segments and Shelters.* Montclair, N.J.: Allanfield, Osman and Co. Publishers, 1976.

Freeman, Richard. *Black Economic Progress After 1964: Who Has Gained and Why?* National Bureau of Economic Research, Working Paper No. 282. Cambridge, Massachusetts, Nov. 1978.

Freeman, Richard. "Changes in the Labor Market for Black Americans, 1948-72." *Brookings Papers On Economic Activity* 1 (1973): 67-131.

Freeman, Richard. *Black Elite.* New York: McGraw-Hill Book Company, 1976.

Friedman, Barry L., and Hausman, Leonard J. *Work and Welfare Patterns of Low Income Families.* The Florence Heller Graduate School for Advanced Studies in Social Welfare, Brandeis University, 1975.

Garfinkle, Stuart. "Occupation of Women and Black Workers 1962-1974." *The Monthly Labor Review* 98 (Nov. 1975): 25-35.

Gilman, Harry. "Economic Discrimination and Unemployment." *American Economic Review* 55 (Dec. 1965): 1077-1096.

Gilroy, Curtis. "Black and White Unemployment: The Dynamics of the Differential." *Monthly Labor Review* 97 (Feb. 1974): 38-47.

Gilroy, Curtis. *Unemployment in Recessions: Women and Black Workers.* Washington, D.C.: U.S. Department of Labor, April 1977.

Glover, Robert W. "Demonstration Project to Facilitate Entry of Minority Women into Managerial, Professional, and Technical Occupations." Final Report, Center for the Study of Human Resources, University of Texas, 1976.

Glover, Robert W., and Greenfield, Paula S. "The Minority Women Employment Program: A National Demonstration Project to Facilitate Entry of Minority Women into Managerial, Professional, and Technical Occupations." Final Report, Center for the Study of Human Resources, University of Texas, 1976.

Goodwin, Leonard. *What Has Been Learned From the Work Incentive Program and Related Experiences: A Review of Research with Policy Implications.* Worcester Polytechnic Institute, 1977.

Green, Barbara M. "Upgrading Black Women in the Supervisory Ranks." *Personnel* 46 (Nov.-Dec., 1969): 47-50.

Grossman, Allyson Sherman. *Children of Working Mothers.* Special Labor Force Report No. 205. Bureau of Labor Statistics, March 1976.

Gurin, Patricia. "The Role of Worker Expectancies in the Study of Employment Discrimination." *Women, Minorities and Employment Discrimination,* ed. by P. Wallace and A. LaMond. Lexington, Mass.: Lexington Books, 1977.

Gurin, Patricia, and Epps, Edgar. *Black Consciousness, Identity and Achievement.* New York: John Wiley and Sons, Inc., 1975.

Gurin, Patricia, and Gaylord, Carolyn. "Educational and Occupational Goals of Men and Women at Black Colleges." *Monthly Labor Review,* vol. 99, no. 6 (June 1976): 10–16.

Gwartney, James. "Changes in the Nonwhite/White Income Ratio, 1939-67." *American Economic Review* 60 (Dec. 1970): 872–883.

Gwartney, James. "Discrimination and Income Differentials." *American Economic Review* 60 (June 1970): 396–408.

Hall, Robert E., and Kasten, Richard. "The Relative Occupational Success of Blacks and Whites." *Brookings Papers on Economic Activity* 3 (1973): 781–797.

Hare, Nathan, and Hare, Julia. "Black Woman 1970." *Transaction* 8 (Dec. 1970): 65–68, 90.

Harrison, Bennett. *Education, Training, and the Urban Ghetto.* Baltimore: Johns Hopkins University Press, 1972.

Harrison, Bennett. "Labor Market Structure and the Relationship Between Work and Welfare." Unpublished manuscript, June 1977

Hausman, Leonard J. "The Impact of Welfare on the Work Effort of AFDC Mothers." U.S. President's Commission on Income Maintenance Programs, Technical Studies, 1970.

Haworth, Joan Gustafson. "Changes in the Relative Economic Status of Women From 1960 to 1970." Unpublished study, Florida State University, 1973.

Hayghe, Howard. "Marital and Family Characteristics of the Labor Force in March 1973." *Monthly Labor Review* 97 (April 1974): 21–27.

Hiestand, Dale L. *Economic Growth and Employment Opportunities for Minorities.* New York: Columbia University Press, 1964.

Hill, Robert B. *The Strengths of Black Families.* New York: Emerson-Hall Publishers, Inc., 1972.

Holt, Charles. "Modeling a Segmented Labor Market." *Women, Minorities and Employment Discrimination,* ed. P. Wallace and A. LaMond. Lexington, Mass.: Lexington Books, 1977.

Hudis, Paula M. "Commitment to Work and Wages: Earnings Differences of Black and White Women." *Sociology of Work and Occupations,* vol. 4, no. 2 (May 1977): 123–146.

Jackson, Jacqueline. "Black Women in a Racist Society." *Racism and Mental Health* by Bertham Brown, Bernard Kramer, and Charles Willie. Pittsburgh, Penn.: University of Pittsburgh Press, 1973.

Jackson, Jacqueline. "But Where Are the Men?" *The Black Scholar* 3 (Dec. 1971): 30–41.

Jackson, Larry R. "Welfare Mothers and Black Liberation." *The Black Scholar* (April 1970): 31–37.

Johnson, Beverly L. "Women Who Head Families, 1970–1977: Their Numbers Rose, Income Lagged." *Monthly Labor Review,* vol. 101, no. 2 (Feb. 1978): 32–37. (See also Beverly Johnson McEaddy.)

Jones, Barbara. "The Contribution of Black Women to the Incomes of Black Families: An Analysis of the Labor Force." Unpublished dissertation, June 1973.

Kiefer, Nicholas. *The Economic Benefits from Manpower Training Programs.* Technical Analysis Paper No. 43, Office of the Assistant Secretary for Policy, Evaluation, and Research, Washington, D.C., November 1976.

Ladner, Joyce. *Tomorrow's Tomorrow: The Black Woman.* Garden City, N.Y.: Doubleday, 1971.

LaRue, Linda. "Black Liberation and Women's Lib." *Transaction* 8 (Dec. 1970): 59–64.

LaRue, Linda. "The Black Movement and Women's Liberation." *The Black Scholar* 1 (May 1970): 36–47.

Leibowitz, Arleen. "Education and the Allocation of Women's Time." *Education, Income and Human Behavior,* ed. F. Thomas Juster, Jr., pp. 171–197. New York: McGraw-Hill Book Company, 1975.

Leon, Carol, and Bednarzik, Robert W. "A Profile of Women On Part-Time Schedules." *Monthly Labor Review,* vol. 101, no. 10 (October 1978): 3–12.

Lerner, G. *Black Women in White America: A Documentary History.* New York: Pantheon, 1972.

Levy, Frank S. "How Big Is the American Underclass?" *The Income Dynamics of the Poor* by Frank Levy, et al. Berkeley, California: Institute of Business and Economic Research, University of California, January 1977.

Levitan, Sar A.; Johnson, William B.; and Taggart, Robert. *Still A Dream.* Cambridge, Mass.: Harvard University Press, 1975.

Lewis, Hylan G., et al. *Improving Employment Opportunities for Female Black Teenagers in New York City.* R&D Monograph 47. U.S. Department of Labor, Washington, D.C., 1977.

Loury, Glenn. "A Dynamic Theory of Racial Income Differences." *Women, Minorities and Employment Discrimination,* eds. Phyllis A. Wallace and Annette LaMond, pp. 153–186. Lexington, Mass.: Lexington Books, 1977.

Mae, Verta. *Thursdays and Every Other Sunday Off.* New York: Doubleday, 1972

Malcolm, S. H.; Hall, P. Q.; and Brown, J. W. "The Double Bind: The Price of Being a Minority Woman in Science," American Association for the Advancement of Science, Report No. 76-R-3. Washington, D.C., April 1976.

Malcolm, S. H.; Hall, P. Q.; and Brown, J. W. "Labor Force Participation and Unemployment: A Review of Recent Evidence." *Prosperity and Unemployment,* R. A. Gordon and M. S. Gordon, eds., pp. 73–112. New York: John Wiley & Sons, 1966.

Marshall, Ray, and Christin, Virgil, eds. *Employment of Blacks in the South.* Austin: University of Texas Press, 1978.

McEaddy, Beverly Johnson. "Women Who Head Families: A Socioeconomic Analysis." *Monthly Labor Review* 99 (June 1976): 3–9. (See also Beverly L. Johnson.)

Mincer, Jacob. "Labor Force Participation of Married Women: A Study of Labor Supply." *Aspects of Labor Economics.* National Bureau of Economic Research Conference Series, No. 14, pp. 63–105. Princeton, N.J.: Princeton University Press, 1962.

Mooney, James D. "Housing Segregation, Negro Employment, and Metropolitan Decentralization: An Alternative Perspective." *Quarterly Journal of Economics* 83 (May 1969): 299–311.

Morrison, Toni. "What the Black Woman Thinks about Women's Lib." *The New York Times Magazine,* August 22, 1971.

Munnell, Alicia H. "The Economic Experience of Blacks: 1964–1974." *New England Economic Review,* Federal Reserve Bank of Boston, Jan. 17, 1978, pp. 5–18.

Murray, Pauli. "The Liberation of Black Women." *Voices of the New Feminism,* ed. Mary Lou Thompson. Boston: Beacon Press, 1971.

Murray, Pauli. "The Negro Woman's Stake in the Equal Rights Amendment." *Harvard Civil Rights-Civil Liberties Law Review* 6 (March 1971): 253–259.

National Commission for Manpower Policy. *CETA: An Analysis of the Issues,* Special Report No. 23, May 1978.

National Commission for Manpower Policy. *Women's Changing Roles at Home and on the Job,* Special Report No. 26, Sept. 1978.

National Commission on Employment and Unemployment Statistics. *Counting the Labor Force,* Washington, D.C., Sept. 1979.

National Committee on Household Employment. *Final Report of the Experimental and Demonstration Projects.* Springfield, Va.: National Technical Information Service, 1971.

Noble, Jeanne L. "The American Negro Women." *The American Negro Reference Book,* ed. John P. Davis. Englewood Cliffs, N.J.: Prentice-Hall, Inc., 1966.

Noble, Jeanne L. *The Negro Woman's College Education.* New York: Teachers College, Columbia University Press, 1956.

Oaxaca, Ronald L. "The Persistence of Male-Female Earnings Differentials." *The Distribution of Economic Well-Being,* ed. Thomas Juster. Cambridge, Mass.: Ballinger Publishing Company, 1977.

Oaxaca, Ronald L. "Sex Discrimination in Wages." *Discrimination in Labor Markets,* ed. Orley Ashenfelter and Albert Rees, pp. 124–151. Princeton, N.J.: Princeton University Press, 1973.

Osterman, Paul. "An Empirical Study of Labor Market Segmentation." *Industrial and Labor Relations Review* 4 (July 1975): 508–523.

Parker, Seymour, and Kleiner, Robert J. "Characteristics of Negro Mothers in Single-Headed Households." *Journal of Marriage and Family* 28 (November 1966).

Parnes, Herbert, et al. *Years for Decision: A Longitudinal Study of the Educational and Labor Market Experience of Young Women.* Manpower Research Monographs No. 24, vols. I-IV. Washington, D.C.: U.S. Department of Labor, 1971, 1973, 1974, 1978. (See also *Dual Careers.*)

Parnes, Herbert S. "Labor Force Participation and Labor Mobility." *A Review of Industrial Relations Research,* vol. 1, pp. 33. Madison, Wisc.: Industrial Relations Research Association, 1970.

Perry, C., Anderson, B., et al. *The Impact of Government Manpower Programs.* Philadelphia: University of Pennsylvania Press, 1975.

Puryear, Gwendolyn R., and Mednick, Martha S. "Black Militancy, Affective Attachment, and the Fear of Success in Black College Women." *Journal of Consulting and Clinical Psychology* 42 (1974): 263-266.

Reagan, Barbara. "Comments on Ashenfelter and Heckman Paper." Unpublished manuscript, Workshop on Equal Employment Opportunities, MIT, January 1974.

Reid, Inez Smith. *Together Black Women.* New York: Emerson Hall Publishing Company, 1972.

Ross, Heather L., and Sawhill, Isabel V. *Time of Transition, The Growth of Families Headed by Women.* Washington, D.C.: The Urban Institute, 1975.

Ruggles, Nancy D., and Ruggles, Richard. "The Anatomy of Earnings Behavior." *The Distribution of Economic Well-Being,* ed. Thomas Juster. Cambridge, Mass.: Ballinger Publishing Company, 1977.

Sawers, Larry. "Urban Poverty and Labor Force Participation." *American Economic Review* 62 (June 1972): 414-431.

Smith, James P. "The Convergence to Racial Equality in Women's Wages." Report No. P-6026. Santa Monica, Calif.: RAND, March 1978.

Smith, James P., and Welch, Finis R. "Black-White Male Earnings and Employment: 1960-1970." Report No. R-1666-Dol. Santa Monica, Calif.: RAND, June 1975.

Smith, Ralph E., and Holt, Charles C. "A Job Search Turnover Analysis of the Black-White Unemployment Ratio." *Proceedings of the Twenty-Third Annual Meeting,* Industrial Relations Research Association Series, Dec. 1970, pp. 76-86.

Smith, Ralph E. *Projecting The Size of the Female Labor Force: What Makes a Difference?* Working Paper 3617-010. Washington, D.C.: The Urban Institute, August 1977.

Smith, Ralph E. *The Impact of Macroeconomic Conditions on Employment Opportunities for Women.* U.S. Congress, Joint Economic Committee, 1977.

Sorkin, Alan L. "Education, Occupation, and Income of Nonwhite Women," *The Journal of Negro Education* (Fall 1972): 343-351.

Spring, William; Harrison, Bennett; and Victorisz, Thomas. "Crisis of the Underemployed." *The New York Times Magazine,* November 5, 1972.

Stanford Research Institute, Center for the Study of Welfare Policy. *A Model of the Effect of Income Maintenance on Rates of Marital Dissolution: Evidence from the Seattle and Denver Income Maintenance Experiments,* Research Memorandum 44, February 1979.

Stein, Robert L. "The Economic Status of Families Headed by Women." *Monthly Labor Review* 93 (December 1970): 3–10.

Stewart, Charles T., Jr. *Low-Wage Workers In An Affluent Society.* Chicago: Nelson Hall Company, 1974.

Strober, Myra R. "Economic Aspects of Child Care." *American Women Workers In A Full Employment Economy.* Joint Economic Committee, Congress of the United States, Washington, D.C., 1977.

Sweet, James. *Women in the Labor Force.* New York: Seminar Press, 1973.

Thurow, Lester. *Generating Inequality.* New York: Basic Books, 1975.

Thurow, Lester. "The Indirect Evidence of Government Expenditures." Unpublished document, Jan. 1979.

Treiman, Donald J., and Terrell, Kermit. "Sex and the Process of Status Attainment: A Comparison of Working Women and Men." *American Sociological Review* 40 (1975): 174–200.

Trimble, M. K. *Final Report of the National Pilot Program on Household Employment.* Springfield, Va.: National Technical Information Service, 1971.

U.S. Civil Service Commission. *Equal Employment Opportunity Statistics.* Washington, D.C., November 1977.

U.S. Department of Commerce, Bureau of the Census. Census of the Population: 1970. *Subject Reports.* Final Report PC(2)-1B, *Negro Population.*

U.S. Department of Commerce, Bureau of the Census. Census of Population: 1970. *Subject Reports.* Final Report PC(2)-8B, *Earnings by Occupation and Education, 1970.*

U.S. Department of Commerce, Bureau of the Census. *Characteristics of the Low-Income Population: 1971-1976.* Current Population Reports, Series P-60, No. 86, 91, 98, 102, 106, 115.

U.S. Department of Commerce, Bureau of the Census. *Differences Between Incomes of White and Negro Families by Work Experience of Wife and Region: 1970, 1969 and 1959.* Current Population Reports, Series P-23, No. 39, December 1971.

U.S. Department of Commerce, Bureau of the Census. *Illustrative Projections of Money Income Size Distributions for Families and Unrelated Individuals.* Current Population Reports. Special Studies, Series P-23, No. 47, February 1974.

U.S. Department of Commerce, Bureau of the Census. *Money Income of Families and Persons in the United States.* Current Population Reports, Series P-60, No. 101, 105, 114.

U.S. Department of Commerce, Bureau of the Census. *Supplementary Report on the Low-Income Population: 1966-1972.* Current Population Reports, Consumer Income, Series P-60, No. 95. July 1974.

U.S. Department of Commerce, Bureau of the Census, Social and Economic Statistics Administration. *Female Family Heads.* Current Population Reports, Special Studies, Series P-23, No. 50, July 1974.

U.S. Department of Labor. *Dual Careers: A Longitudinal Study of Labor Market Experience of Women.* Manpower Research Monograph 21. (See also *Dual Careers.*)

U.S. Department of Labor, Bureau of Labor Statistics. *Earnings and Other Characteristics of Organized Workers,* Report 556, May 1977.

U.S. Department of Labor, Bureau of Labor Statistics. *Marital and Family Characteristics of the Labor Force: March 1971-1977.* Special Labor Force Reports No. 144, 153, 164, 173, 183, 206, 216.

U.S. Department of Labor, Bureau of Labor Statistics. *Work Experience of the Population in 1970-1976.* Special Reports 141, 162, 171, 181, 190, 201.

U.S. Department of Labor, Employment Standards Administration. *Private Household Workers.* Washington, D.C., 1974.

U.S. Department of Labor, Employment and Training Administration, *Employment and Training Report of the President,* various years.

U.S. Department of Labor, Employment and Training Administration. *Research Uses of the National Longitudinal Surveys.* Washington, D.C., 1979.

U.S. Department of Labor, Employment and Training Administration. *Income Inequality and Employment.* R&D Monograph 66. Washington, D.C., 1978.

U.S. Department of Labor, Women's Bureau. *Negro Women in the Population and in the Labor Force.* Washington, D.C.: U.S. Government Printing Office, 1968.

U.S. Department of Labor, Women's Bureau. *1975 Handbook on Women Workers* (Bulletin 297). Washington, D.C.: U.S. Government Printing Office, 1975.

U.S. Department of Labor, Women's Bureau, *Minority Women Workers: A Statistical Overview,* rev. Washington, D.C.: U.S. Government Printing Office, 1977.

Vroman, Wayne. "Changes in Black Workers' Relative Earnings: Evidence from the 1960's." *Patterns of Racial Discrimination,* vol. 2, ed. George M. von Furstenberg, et al., pp. 167-169. Lexington, Mass.: Lexington Books, 1974.

Wachtel, Howard, and Betsey, Charles. "Employment at Low Wage." *Review of Economics and Statistics* (May 1972): 121-129.

Wachter, Michael L. "Primary and Secondary Labor Markets: A Critique of the Dual Approach." *Brookings Papers On Economic Activity* 3 (1974): 637-693.

Waldman, Elizabeth, and Whitmore, Robert. "Children of Working Mothers, March 1973." *Monthly Labor Review* 97 (May 1974): 50-58.

Wallace, Phyllis A. *Affirmative Action and Increased Labor Force Participation of Women.* Sloan School Working Paper, April 1979.

Wallace, Phyllis A. *Pathways to Work: Unemployment Among Black Teenage Females.* Lexington, Mass.: Lexington Books, 1974.

Wallace, Phyllis A., and LaMond, Annette. *Women, Minorities and Employment Discrimination.* Lexington, Mass.: Lexington Books, 1977.

Weiss, L., and Williamson, J. G. "Black Education, Earnings, and Inter-regional Migration: Some New Evidence." *American Economic Review* 62 (June 1972): 372-383.

Weiss, Randall. "The Effect of Education on the Earnings of Blacks and Whites." *Review of Economics and Statistics* 52 (May 1970): 150-159.

Welch, Finis. "Black-White Differences in Returns to Schooling." *American Economic Review* 63 (December 1973): 893-907.

Weston, Peter J., and Mednick, Martha T. "Race, Social Class and the Motive to Avoid Success in Women." *Journal of Cross-Cultural Psychology* 1 (September 1970): 382-391.

Whiting, Jack E., Jr. "Dichotomous Market Structure and the Labor Force Participation of the Urban Poor." Center for the Study of Human Resources, University of Texas, August 1974.

Williams, Robert George. *Public Assistance and Work Effort: The Labor Supply of Low-Income Female Heads of Household.* Industrial Relations Section, Princeton University, 1975.

Wool, Harold. *The Labor Supply for Lower Level Occupations.* New York: Praeger, 1976.

Index